Basil has over 60 years of sea experience. The last 6 years encompass long-distance solo sailing, including 3 Jester Challenges and an Atlantic Circuit.

Basil settled in his adopted England in 1964, married, had children, divorced and remarried. It was his second wife who, after retirement and in order to occupy his time, suggested that he bought a boat, as he no longer taught sailing or involved himself with the Boat Show. She subsequently regretted her suggestion, as this started his solo career, which kept him away from home for long periods, sailing long distances in a very small boat, which some might consider far too small for such sailing ventures.

Basil lived his dream and he considers himself privileged to have met a number of similar-minded sailors and lucky to have survived what the elements have thrown at him.

To my lovely wife and friends. Thank you. Without your support and patience, I would have never achieved my dream and without whose help this book never have been completed.

Basil Panakis

JESTER CHALLENGE AND BEYOND

SMALL BOAT ATLANTIC CROSSING ON A BUDGET

AUSTIN MACAULEY PUBLISHERS™
LONDON · CAMBRIDGE · NEW YORK · SHARJAH

Copyright © Basil Panakis (2019)

The right of Basil Panakis to be identified as author of this work has been asserted by him in accordance with section 77 and 78 of the Copyright, Designs and Patents Act 1988.

All rights reserved. No part of this publication may be reproduced, stored in a retrieval system, or transmitted in any form or by any means, electronic, mechanical, photocopying, recording, or otherwise, without the prior permission of the publishers.

Any person who commits any unauthorised act in relation to this publication may be liable to criminal prosecution and civil claims for damages.

A CIP catalogue record for this title is available from the British Library.

ISBN 9781528925778 (Paperback)
ISBN 9781528964432 (ePub e-book)

www.austinmacauley.com

First Published (2019)
Austin Macauley Publishers Ltd
25 Canada Square
Canary Wharf
London
E14 5LQ

It took some time to put down my thoughts and recollections which my wife, Jackie, had to decipher, put in some order and proofread. Steve and Lynn, my next-door neighbours, were my next call for proofreading of the manuscript and they came back with their corrections. Likewise, Len had a go and also kindly let me use one of his photos he took of JABA at the start of our Jester Newport Challenge 2016.

The biggest thank goes to Jake, who ceaselessly advised and humoured me along the way. The cover changed upon his insistence. Roger very willingly scripted the foreword after reading the whole book. He also contributed to the front cover.

At the start of the Jester Newport Challenge 2018 in Plymouth, I asked Ewen if he would like to write something about the book and he generously obliged.

Also to all those knowingly or otherwise who contributed by supporting me in all my trips and towards the production of this book.

Table of Contents

Foreword	**13**
Chapter 1	**17**
What Is It in a Name?	
Chapter 2	**24**
Preparing the Boat for Solo-Sailing	
Inside	*24*
Outside	*26*
Electronics and Instruments	*29*
Chapter 3	**32**
Jester Azores Challenge 2012	
Now a few gems from the log book entries.	*38*
Chapter 4	**40**
Jester Challenge 2014	
Chapter 5	**69**
Jester Azores Challenge 2016	
Chapter 6	**75**
Atlantic Circuit – Jester Challenge Beyond	
Madeira	*77*
Lanzarote	*80*

Cape Verde	*85*
St Lucia	*89*
St Lucia, April 2017	*94*
Antigua 17:00.9 N 61:46.8 W	*96*
Antigua to the Azores	*100*
Praia da Vitoria.	*104*
The last leg, Azores to Southampton	*108*

Chapter 7 — 111

Reminiscing – Fastnet Races

Sailing School	*118*
Boat Shows	*126*
Orchids	*128*

Chapter 8 — 131

Jester Symposiums, Dreamers and Pogrom

Jester Challenge and Beyond
Small Boat Atlantic Circuit on a Budget

Foreword

The Jester Challenge, with its premise of taking ocean voyaging, and in particular, the crossing of the North Atlantic, back to a simple and seamanlike exercise in modest boats with modest skippers, has a constant capacity to amaze and delight. It has drawn together a disparate collection of odd-balls, united by a belief in self-reliance, simplicity and camaraderie. It has nurtured and transformed many a skipper from hesitant tyro to quietly competent old salt. Under the unceasingly wise guidance of its visionary mentor, Ewen Southby-Tailyour, it has taken on its own organic life-force, and so seems to grow and expand month on month, year on year.

The creative impulse generated by the Jester Challenge is by no means confined to the sailing itself. Not only have skippers found a congenial structure in which to develop their sea-going skills, many have also found it to be a catalyst to self-expression and self-examination. Participation in the Jester Challenge 'movement' has encouraged a number of skippers to find their voice and tell their story. And what stories they are!

This extraordinary reminiscence by Basil Panakis perfectly illustrates the power of the Jester Challenge to ignite hidden fires. It also illustrates the unlikely confluence of even more unlikely personalities on which the Jester Challenge thrives. Consider this: Basil was born into the Greek community in Istanbul during the time when the always-troubled relationship between Greece and Turkey was at one of its lowest ebbs. As a child he witnessed the violent pogroms against the Greek community and eventually had to flee, perhaps literally, for his life.

Here is his story. It is told simply, without the least trace of literary guile, without any self-conscious attempt at stylistic subtlety, and therein lies its own particular power and merit. Considering that it is also written in what for Basil is his second language, it is an impressive achievement. We may as well be sat next to Basil in the pub as he tells his tale, his anecdotes tumbling out willy-nilly, a thousand Toms, Dicks and Harrys coming and going in a breath-taking twirl of walk-on characters. Shining through is Basil's indomitable will, his sense of humour and his willingness to accept misfortune with little more than a shrug of the shoulders. It is, therefore, a tale from which we can all learn.

Roger D. Taylor
Jester Challenge and Beyond

Basil Panakis had a dream, although, perhaps at the time, he did not recognise it!

Despite being a veteran of Fastnet races, sailing, school instructing and charter yacht skippering – while demonstrably dedicated to the 'seamanship, not showmanship' school of philosophy – he had never sailed single-handed until 2012. Then he heard of the Jester Azores Challenge due to take place that summer and, unexpectedly, caught up with his dream. He has never looked back.

Now, after three 'Jesters', and other notable single-handed voyages, Basil has come to epitomise what the Jester Challenge is all about and, through highly entertaining – and, importantly, instructive – blogs, he continues to fulfil his vision. In doing so, he encourages others to 'let go' of the nautically-normal and the mundane, for, quite simply, Basil is one of the Jester Challenge's leading lights, encompassing, as he does in his voyages, all the finer virtues required of this most purist of small-yacht endeavours.

Newcomers to our way of life can do no better than be amused at, be entertained by and be encouraged through Basil's life: a life made even more unusual by his far-from-normal early struggles in a 'foreign' country.

Yachtsmen's stories, unless of genuine significance, tend not to be 'bestsellers', which, in Basil's case, would be a pity, for he has an inspirational story to tell and he tells it in an engrossing, uplifting and readable manner.

Read *Jester Challenge and Beyond…* and perhaps you, too, will be encouraged to dream.

Ewen Southby-Tailyour

Jester Challenge and Beyond

Chapter 1
What Is It in a Name?

"The essence of being human is that one does not seek perfection." – George Orwell

I thought of calling/naming the book 'Spur of Jester', as it is the Jester Challenge that converted me really to a solo sailor. The book will follow and go beyond my videos as it will explain and enhance the uploaded videos. Jake suggested that it should be called 'Jester Challenge Beyond', as it would encapsulate more than the original idea of a Jester Challenge participation.

Up to joining the Jester Challenge, all of my sailing was in company with others. Either I would crew for a skipper or later would be as an RYA instructor for over ten years. My involvement with the sea started when I was 10 by helping my dad get on with his fishing back home. I cannot say that I enjoyed getting up at the crack of dawn to go fishing, though, we had some very challenging and memorable experiences. I preferred my sleep. My brothers, both younger than me, got hooked on fishing and carried on even after our father's death.

My experience as a solo sailor was very minimal, a couple of short distance sailing school yacht deliveries. Even after buying my boat mainly I had a helping hand on board. I would move the boat say from Southampton to Gosport and vice versa solo as I belonged to two clubs based one in each location and that was it. The motivation to go solo came from the Jester Challenge.

I was very interested to go to the Azores long before I heard about the Jester Challenge, even though again not as a solo adventure. It was the whale hunting and the adventures associated with it. Influenced from films and books I had a desire to go to these wind-blown volcanic outcrops. More recently of Brian, who skippered a delivery from the Caribbean to UK via the Azores. Particularly, when John and Nicola expressed a desire to buy a residence there (Flores) at pre EU-prices while cruising in the Archipelago.

Jester Challenge is a biennial event for yachts under 9.1m (30ft). Its origins lie in the Observer Single-handed Trans-Atlantic Race (OSTAR) started by Blondie Hasler in 1960. Sir Francis Chichester won that first race. But as that race became more commercialised, owners of smaller boats set up their own Corinthian event named after Jester, the custom designed junk-rigged Folkboat that Hasler sailed to the second place in the inaugural OSTAR.

In the words of our guru and organiser Ewen Southby-Tailyour: 'The Jester Challenge fills a gap – satisfies a desire – and exists on the understanding that everyone has the right to sail across an ocean single-handed and 'in company' without submitting themselves to entrance fees and rules, other than those governing common sense and good seamanship. There is no organising committee, no one has a duty of care to the competitors other than the skippers to themselves, their dependants and other seafarers.'

The Jester Challenge has historically alternated between the Jester Azores Challenge, from Plymouth to Ponta Delgada originally which then moved to Praia da Vitoria, Terceira as time progressed and the Jester Challenge to Newport Rhode Island, USA. After the 2012 JAC, Nick started to organise an in between shorter race for the odd years, thus the Baltimore (Ireland) race evolved and taken over by Ewen as part of the Jester set up, to coincide with the Baltimore Pirate weekend. First one took place in 2013. A weekend of events remembering in an entertaining way one of the most sensational events in Baltimore's colourful past and one which made the village a focus of international attention – the attack by Barbary corsairs known as 'the Sack of Baltimore'. However, the Algerians were by no means the only pirates operating in the waters around Baltimore. The bays and inlets of Roaring Water Bay were the principal European base for pirates of many different nationalities who plied their trade right across the Atlantic to the Caribbean.

I retired at sixty and got married before my 60th birthday as Jackie did not want to marry a pensioner. After retirement, I decided to go around the world before I became too old to travel. I had done a number of long distance trips after my divorce but as I was still working these trips had to fit with my employment. In 1997/98, I combined the Christmas holiday period with extra leave and managed to go for an overland trip from Nairobi to Johannesburg in the back of a lorry over a period of 6 weeks. That was my second and longest trip in Africa. So, I was not really new to travelling alone but not solo. This came with the world travel that lasted 7 months and nearly caused a second divorce.

On my return, I thought it would be a good idea to keep my hand in sailing and purchase a small boat with a mind to sailing around the Solent with the occasional trip across to France. I had a number of dinghies in the past which I enjoyed sailing and passed on my enthusiasm to others. This boat would need to have a cabin, a place to sleep. Ken had a small boat where you could not stand up in it, a bucket and over the side job. I made a list of 25 to 30 footers and started looking, when John told me that Colin was on a look out too, so we joined forces and had a few trips around the country to look for suitable boats. Eventually, this came to a stop as nothing really came up as a suitable boat or price wise. There were plenty of boats around of course but not at our price or spec requirements. I remember Colin not wanting a long keel because of its reversing ability. Do not forget that it is not only buying the boat, you have to think of the berthing and maintenance expenditure. I took Brian with me on one trip to Essex to look at a steel boat, where the owner was using me as a lever to extract more money from a prospective buyer. We went all the way there to be told only when we arrived there that the boat was sold only minutes before. I had phoned the seller only half an hour before our arrival to ask if everything was fine and he had said OK. Brian was more furious than me. I saw it as one of those things. I learned about keel cooling and a lot of other things in the process.

I remember going on a demo with Colin out of Gosport on Trevor's boat. It would have been an ideal boat, Van der Stad design, but we couldn't agree on the price. A year or so later, Trevor phoned me and offered me his boat at the original price I wanted to pay. It was too late as by then I had purchased the Contest 25 mark II in January 2007.

In 2014 on my first day back at work at the Docks, after my return from the Jester Challenge, Tony came up to me and asked, "When are you publishing your book?" I said that I was not planning anything and his comment was, "We all have a book in us." This of course was on the strength of Tony reading my blog which included not only the daily sailing experiences but also recollections and reminiscences of the past, be it sailing or otherwise.

During the Jester Symposium of 2015 in Ipswich, Eric's partner Marie-Odile during our meal told me how much she liked my blog and that she was looking forward each day to the next one. Out of curiosity I asked her what exactly she liked. The diversity of the experiences and stories you covered.

So, let's get on with the purchase of the boat.

It was on eBay that I saw the ad for a Contest 25 in Plymouth. I probably still have the paperwork somewhere. It looked good on paper and the price was within what I wanted to spend. This was going to be the first Contest I was going to view. I called the seller and we made arrangements for viewing. The boat was on a trot mooring, I asked how I was to recognise him and he told me that he drove a Skoda, when I asked him what it looked like, he said a Mercedes!

When I arrived at the quay, I could see that they were already on the boat. The son came and picked me up in an inflatable that had a slow puncture. I liked the boat and within say 20 minutes I agreed to buy her after some price haggling.

Had it been with an agent it would have been £7500 to £8000. The boat had not been updated but it looked clean and well kept. The owner, a taxi driver, used it like a floating caravan for his family and grand-children and had not done much due to health problems. Apparently, his heart rate was up to 250 and they stopped and restarted his heart a number of times at the hospital. I paid an over the top deposit and left. Two weeks later, I had a mishap myself but as I did not want to lose my deposit I carried on with the transaction. What he did not tell me was that he had cancelled the insurance the moment the contract was signed, though he had told me that it had another month or so to run. I found this out when I went to renew the insurance. Second problem was with the trot mooring, I phoned the Council and made arrangements, but as I was prevented from leaving the mooring as arranged they came upon me like a ton of bricks. Things get delayed at times at sea.

I made friends with Vic who had a lovely house by the quay in Oreston who kept an eye on my boat while I was not there. He had a lovely yacht himself on a swinging mooring, a border collie with a red and white neck scarf. I travelled a few times down and stayed on board. I spent a night in the quarter berth once and, although, it was frosty outside I was fine in that coffin of a place. I had to splash the cockpit and deck with sea water in order to get rid of the ice.

The only battery was under the starboard berth. The previous owner used to take the battery home, charge it and bring it back. This battery served for all purposes. I made arrangements with Vic for an electrician to come and install a second battery as well as an isolator switch. On my next trip down I found out that the isolator switch did not power the instrument panel. Down came the electrician again and made the necessary connections/re-connections.

Spring was coming by then and it was time to move the boat to Southampton. I spoke to Graham of Itchen Marine in Southampton, as at that time I did not belong to any club for a mooring.

I got in touch with one of my ex sailing students, John, who joined me for the move. Despite the weather not being helpful, 30 knots on the nose we still set sail. The furling headsail would not unfurl, this was the first problem we encountered. I went on deck and disconnected the sheets and unrolled the sail by hand…then reconnected the sail. This eventually temporarily cured the problem. We decided to call into Salcome. The next day was John's birthday. I tried to find a rigger to sort out the problem with the furling gear, to no avail. Next, we decided to move to Dartmouth but the head winds were a problem. The topping lift was a fixed stainless steel wire allowing no adjustment so I decided to take the D shackle off and play with the main sheet. This caused a reap above the second reef. We were snookered, either get back to Salcome or to Plymouth. We chose the latter. The sail was repaired there, a terrible job done without a patch by someone who had a loft and called himself sailmaker. Obviously, he did not have repeat customers or recommendations. He must have relied on passing trade. By this time, we decided to go alongside and give the boat a scrub. To our surprise we found at least 5 to 6 inches growth of mussels on the keel. After that the boat was unbelievably fast under engine as we were going for a refuel. The weather had settled and we had to resort to motoring for most part of the way especially around Portland Bill. We arrived in Southampton on Sunday after a week's sailing.

I eventually attained a half tide berth, at the American Warf marina. John some time later phoned me and asked whether he could become my partner in the ownership of JABA. I had already registered and changed the boat's name from VEGA III to JABA, which stands for part of our names **JA**ckie **BA**sil, and nothing to do with Spielberg's film.

One of the first things was to get the boat out and strip all the antifouling by having it soft blasted. Some blistering was noted but nothing to worry about. I took all the old instruments out and had AIS and Navtex fitted. Log and echo sounder replaced the older instruments. The compass that came with the boat was of the removable kind, so a new pair was put in the cockpit bulkhead where you could read the reciprocal course from the respective berths. Had the riggers around to check the rig and they were a bit over enthusiastic in tuning it. They cracked one of the mast supporting beams. The mast is deck stepped and was resting over the main bulkhead, which had two beams either side of it, to reinforce the deck head and bulkhead and transfer the loads down the door frame to the keel. This crack was not visible and I had not noticed it, however as I was photographing parts of the boat I noticed it on the computer. I took off the offending beam and had a replacement made in mild steel, one inch thick. Meanwhile, according to Simon, I needed to address the chain plates, as these in many instances are the culprits of dismasting. I designed new plates to fit on the main cabin side of the bulkhead and the five bolts holding the original chain plate on the heads side were replaced with longer ones thus sandwiching the bulkhead. In addition, this stainless-steel chain plate incorporated an ear like extension with bigger bolts securing it straight through the bulkhead. According to Glen, each chain plate can take 20000 lbs weight. Either side of the companion way grab handles were fitted thus facilitating our way in and out.

We did a couple of trips to France that summer to test the boat. So, a life-raft was bought together with a number of clip on head sails. A three-year-old fully battened main was purchased and Sarah made our new main from that.

During the crossing, we hit a large patch of seaweed and our speed dropped from 5 to 3 knots. We struggled into Cherbourg. I checked with the marina which wanted 40 euro to lift and clear the prop, a bargain, as it would have cost a lot more back home. However, I had a huge hunting knife which I tied and taped to the broom handle and undertook the clearing job. I removed all items from the port cockpit locker and placed on the starboard side deck, moved items from down below too and I leaned myself over the side holding the stays while John C cleared the shaft and prop.

On the way back, it was still calm and one of us stayed in the bows directing the other away from the weeds.

During the second trip to Cherbourg the weather picked up and we made it in the dark. So, we moored in the middle pontoon and spent the night there and in the morning, we moved into a visitor's berth. DUET was in the middle pontoon too. The couple next to us in their huge boat thought that we had just arrived and were very impressed as the wind had increased to gale force by then. I just said it was lumpy and left it at that. This time though we had a different problem, our engine would not start. So, John went and got the biggest battery he could find and brought it back. Its weight almost killed him, what killed me was the price £175, in 2007. When we came back I had Graham (retired ex RK Marine) around who took the alternator home and found a dry joint inside. So, we saved some money this way by not having to buy a replacement alternator.

I joined Netley Cliff Sailing Club as it was cheaper to keep the boat there in winter. For say in those days probably £80, I could keep the boat on dry land for 6 months. I had to buy a second-hand trolley from a member who had moved his boat to POG. Initially, we bought a proper cradle which we fitted on the trolley but we thought to have something more permanent, so we sold the cradle and bought some Acrow props and Steve welded these on the trolley. This arrangement still works.

Also bought ground tackle and put the boat on a swinging mooring for a couple of years or so. Portsmouth Offshore Group was another South Coast Civil Service sailing club, so I joined that one too. I managed to get a trot mooring in Wicor, which I never used and swapped it for a swinging mooring by Burrow Island. John and I always entertained the idea of going to go to the Azores together. After all, he did a couple of Fastnet Races with me.

However, the relationship with John came to a dead end and I bought his share back. His idea was to sell the boat and split the proceeds. Not an option for me after all the effort I had put in the boat. He was more or less a sleeping partner by then, not a very good investment for him as he hardly came down to sail it due to work and family commitments.

So far, all this expenditure was to bring the boat up to date and make it pleasure to sail.

After regaining full ownership again, I changed details with SSR and I had a Survey carried out in preparation for some solo sailing. The surveyor found a few details that needed some attention which I sorted out (for example a bolt holding the forestay which Simon changed to a clevis pin). I could not really believe that the surveyor wanted to put an insurance value of £16000 to the boat. I said £14000 may be a better option, and when I relayed this to Simon, his comments were that the price reflected all the modifications, renewals and the state of the boat.

Chapter 2
Preparing the Boat for Solo-Sailing

"Try a thing you haven't done three times. Once, to get over the fear of doing it. Twice, to learn how to do it. And a third time to figure out whether you like it or not."

– Virgil Thomson

Inside

Although, one of the mast supports was replaced this time I had a further stainless-steel beam support made which was bolted through to the mild steel beam encapsulating the existing wooden beam and the bulkhead. This arrangement had extensions which were bolted through the door supports that spread the load to the keel.

I found that the wooden handholds in the cabin were too short for the purpose, so I had a stainless-steel hand hold made from bulkhead to bulkhead. Later I made a second one for the port side too. When I installed the first radar I mounted the screen on the starboard side hand hold, on an arm that would enable me to move the screen to be viewed from down below or swung out by the companionway so that could be viewed from the cockpit. Before JAC 2016, I sold this Radar to Bob and purchased a new chart plotter (number 3) which acted as radar screen too (MFD). I could have the chart with the AIS and radar overlay all together. All this arrangement again was mounted on a swinging arm made to measure.

Additionally, extra lines were secured as handholds to stop me being thrown about in the cabin. Even so, on one occasion, I was thrown from the companionway down to the port side and badly hurt the back of my head. I kept on saying to myself, 'Do not close your eyes and go to sleep as you may not wake up.' I managed to survive that rogue wave, but for a number of nights, I could not sleep on my back as my head was really painful.

In the cabin the table was removed and a false floor was made just in front of the companionway steps. Under this board there were two plastic boxes filled with provisions. Also, down below I used to store the inflatable but this eventually was moved and secured on the foredeck. The Jordan drogue still resides down below with a spare 25 litre water container purchased in Cape Verde. This container used to have soap for the laundry industry, most yachts buy and fill these with diesel and strap them along their decks. I keep my spare diesel in two 5 litre containers and two 10 litre containers. In St Lucia, I splashed out and bought a further 10 litre container. In other words, I doubled my range under power. The main diesel tank holds 40 litres.

Richard and Charlie of Ocean Safety were very helpful. Charlie was reluctant to put their name on my boat in case I sank as this would have been bad publicity. I bought quite of few of my electronics, life-raft etc. from them.

The sliding out chart table was removed from it's under the deck fitting. The rail was modified, and the chart table was made to fit above the port bunk. This could slide along the rail and it could swing up on a folding leg. This leg proved to be too short and modifications were discussed with Simon. Nothing happened to this day. The reason being that I put a big plastic box under the chart table, in which I kept delicate items, like the Furuno weather fax, torches, survival food, some clothing, transistor radio, etc.

Simon also changed the instrument panel to something more up to date. A further box was made to accommodate a new additional instrument panel. Simon was quite good in not charging me the full price for the latter.

In the forepeak, I had a number of plastic storage containers full of spares and tools. Some of the containers had water tight boxes stored in them, like a box of courtesy flags, a gas soldering iron as well as a battery operated one, impact drivers, bolts and nuts, D shackles, all sorts of spares, toilet rolls, paper kitchen towels, tea towels, spare trainers, spare sailing boots, wind vane for the self-steering, scuba diving gear, bungs, bolt croppers, screw drivers, battery screw driver, pilot books and charts for France, Portugal, Spain all the way to the Med in case I needed a bolt hole.

The porta-potti was kept there in its box. I had one during the 2014 Jester which I sold upon my return, I purchased another one in Lanzarote as at the time I was planning after the Caribbean to go to the States and do the ICW. I also purchased an incontinence bed cover. However, this did not last the rigours of ocean crossing. I liked Roger's arrangement of see through acrylic covers like those on the sprayhood.

Recently I asked Rene what he thought of the idea and left it to him to sort me out. A brand-new waterproof cover was made for the port bunk and I offered it to Bill to try out, but he declined.

In the quarter berth I kept a cruising chute, a storm jib, the parachute anchor, also a couple of hank-on sails, 30 litres of spare water in two plastic containers, UK charts and three under the bed type plastic boxes with the ship's papers, brochures, paperwork relating to visiting ports, log books, etc.

All the victualling was kept down below too. All meat tins, cans or jars were stored under the starboard berth. In contrast under the port bunk all the non-meat provisions were kept, like peas, beans, spinach, potatoes etc. and tinned fruit. Pasta and rice were kept in an old flares box that's watertight under the forepeak bunks. Fresh food was kept in the plastic boxes under the false floor and on deck. I tried to have at least one fresh fruit a day.

Cereal was kept in the flares box as well as some in the forepeak. Eggs which I boiled were kept by the sink. Initially, I had about a dozen but by Cape Verde I graduated to 18. You have to make sure that you consume the cracked ones first.

Outside

All preparations were an on-going process. I replaced all the standing rigging about a month before departure in 2012 for the Jester Azores Challenge. I had a number of quotes, some involved me taking the boat down to Bursledon, hauling her out etc. Another would have been by Paul who had just been made redundant and would have done it cheaply. Another rigger came around and after promises he did not show up again. The ones I chose were friends from my days with Britannia Sailing. The quote was for say over £450. They were very helpful and had organised for the work to be done at Divers wharf. However, as I was ashore at NCSC we took the mast down at our compound instead, the riggers took the measurements and came back in the afternoon to rig the boat. As a reminder these were the same guys who damaged the supporting beam, some years before. This time some of the rigging was too short and they had to go back to Southampton and get replacement rigging made. They said it would add a bit more to the cost. It was not my mistake. They came back with the new bits and with the help of Danny, Brian and others set the mast up and the riggers tuned it. I called at their workshop few days later and asked for the bill, a temporary employee passed me a pro-forma invoice for a total of £1400. Amazing how this bill escalated. Admittedly, I had asked for some additional items, like a block and tackle for the back stay, and a snap shackle for the main sheet. I got in touch with Chris, the manager, and told him the story and left it with him. It was Chris who actually had given me the quote. I phoned a few more times, he was very busy and the whole thing was forgotten. I did ask him for sponsorship and may be this was his way of dealing with it.

I bought a Hasler SP2 self-steering and had some brackets made in mild steel at Abbey Engineering to support it. Meanwhile, I attended a Jester meeting in London by the Waterloo station. Apparently, this was a regular thing they did on the Thursdays after attending the London Boat Show. That's where I met Roger Taylor with whom I had been corresponding via email, Bill, John, Rory and others, I liked this impromptu meeting. I could join them in Plymouth in May and have some company before the start and afterwards at Terceira.

I like Rene, in Bursledon, who fixes most of my sail/dodger/sprayhood problems nowadays. When I went to ask him for some Hi-Viz strips on my sprayhood he agreed to some yellow bands but didn't want to do orange ones, however Eduardo, his son, agreed with me and incorporated the orange band too. "Now you want a shark too" was Rene's comment and he drew a fish on a yellow background which Eduardo sewed on. It looked very unusual and a number of people actually liked it. At the time I asked Rene if he wanted to put his label on the sprayhood and he declined. When I told him that most people had commented favourably on the design sprayhood he suggested that he should incorporate fishes in all his sprayhoods. I told him that I hold the copyright!

I had Day-Glo orange stick-on vinyl film applied to coachroof and mast, instead of RNLI orange paint as on Andy's BULA in 2012. Reflective tape also applied on the top of the mast to increase visibility. It is ever so easy to find Jaba in a marina. Look up at mast height and there she is. Some of these modifications were carried out in February 2013 just prior to Baltimore Challenge (Ireland).

In order to help the parachute anchor, stay within the fairlead, I opted for two additional cleats and I fed the line through the cleat and then to the fairlead. This way it did not matter whether the line jumped off the fairlead or not, as it was still held at the right angle and did not travel down along the gunnel.

I had a third reef on my main sail, as this sail was really very heavy and I could use it as a trysail too. A very good investment as I found this to be a very efficient way to handle in a gale.

Another improvement was to have a Perspex washboard made. I had asked Simon for a replacement one in wood but he said that his would not be strong enough for my particular use. This enabled me to get light in the cabin and more or less keep it in place most of the time.

I had three anchors on board. A fortress anchor with chain and warp secured down in the foredeck anchor locker. A CQR anchor and a Danforth anchor were in the cockpit locker together with chain and warps.

In order to improve the integrity of the mast an inner removable forestay was installed, and a number of hank-on sails were bought and a storm sail was made by Sarah from the main sail left overs with a big red stuck-on dot. This reminds you of a Japanese flag. I never had the occasion to use this sail in anger.

A stainless-steel frame was made by Ted around the sprayhood that stretched midway on deck. This gave good handhold for the cockpit and when climbing forward along the side decks. Len called it 'Zimmer frame' but I found it invaluable. Additional ropes were attached to it for clambering out from down below and along to the mast.

Talking of lines, there is a line either side that runs from the bow to the stern on the outside just touching the water. If I were to fall overboard the line will give me something to hold on and also be a foothold for climbing on board. There is a further line that runs from the mast to the inner forestay deck attachment. I find this line very convenient to hold and clip on to it too. Roger had the idea which Denis and I adopted too. I use a safety line with an additional hook on a short strop. With that on I cannot go overboard as I am restricted to a foot or so of freedom.

I bought a Jordan's drogue together with the two plates which I had a carpenter come to fix on the boat. This was a two-man job carried out in the middle pontoon in Itchen. We did one side then turned the boat around and did the other side.

This year Bill made me a quite thick and easy to grab 7 metre safety line, one like his, which I will clip on my harness and the other end in the cockpit. "Make sure that you make your way to the fore deck by walking inside the shrouds," he said. If you were to go overboard at least you will end up in the water mid-ship. That's what happened to Bill when he went overboard in rough seas. He wears his at all times even when asleep.

I have attached extended lines to the self-steering so that I can adjust the course from inside the cabin. Dave R in the nineties towed a fender attached to a line, this was a safety feature that if he went overboard he could catch the line and bring himself in, (I was best man at his wedding in 1993). When I had the Hasler I put an extra line over the transom so that if I were to pull this from the water, I could disengage the self-steering and stop the boat. Not much point in being dragged along. I have not figured out anything for the Wind Pilot yet.

Electronics and Instruments

I installed a Marlec 504 Wind Generator on the port quarter, and a couple of semi flexible solar panels on the coachroof. The last two deteriorated with time and as per John Apps' recommendation were replaced with ordinary solid household ones. I had two batteries for the Jester 2012, one for the engine and the other for domestics. I had no problems with the batteries, hardly used the engine to top them up. In fact, after breaking the ignition key I had no access to the engine therefore no charging of batteries per se.

I had a Raymarine autopilot complete with a waterproof cover which I used when preparing the boat to come into port, or when leaving port.

In addition to the AIS receiver I added a transponder too. This way the big ones not only can see me on their radar but also know who I am. I have an RTE (radar target enhancer) up the mast for added security, which is permanently on. For Baltimore I added a Tack Tick wind instrument too. This over the years proved to be a bit temperamental.

You have to move with times, in addition to charts, almanacs and, pilot books I purchased a chart plotter, a Garmin 276C. This was a very popular GPS and Garmin now have made an updated version of it, which unfortunately will not take my old data cards. As I wanted to have the AIS on my chartplotter I invested next on a Garmin 640 (the USA version of our 620). I kept the 276C as a spare, which I put in a Quality Street chocolate tin and kept it in the forepeak (Faraday cage). This was in case I had a lightning strike that destroyed all my instruments. The 276C and 640 had their own dedicated removable batteries, and you could use them away from the boat too.

My first Radar was a Koden, which I replaced with an 18" Garmin HDx that was to go with my new Garmin 751 chart plotter. Now I have 3 chart plotters on board. When I lost power in 2016 I had to rely for a while on the two older ones. In addition, I have a basic GPS, (Street Pilot II Plus) that shows LAT LONG only from the early nineteen nineties. Garmin no longer supports these but Dave P managed to find an internal battery for it and replaced it for me. There is on board a very old Trimble GPS from early nineties too, as a further spare. It appears that I am a hoarder, but you do not know when things could be of use again.

If everything else failed I had a sextant on board too, which I did not use and sold when I came back after JAC 2012.

It appears that every item on board has its story.

On the advice of Tony, I looked for a Furuno Weatherfax on eBay. A breaker's yard in Gujurat had a number of these, some in parts, but for the one they guaranteed they wanted $500, I offered $250 and got it. It was a dud one. Tony had some spare parts and attempted to make a good one but to no avail. I drove down to Plymouth and spent a day with Tony, came back with the Weatherfax and eventually I had a full refund. Another one turned up in Australia and one in Southampton. I told the one in Sydney how to test and it was fine. I visited the guy in Southampton and checked it myself, but he would not accept my offer. He had it on eBay and then after me testing it added that item was in working order and got more money! Eventually, another one turned up somewhere in the West Country which I bought and had it sent to Tony, together with the one from India. Eventually, Tony made a good one that he handed to me in Plymouth just before the Jester Challenge in 2014.

I had a demo given to me locally on SSB radio set up together with the software for my notebook. This worked fine too. I used this for downloading the weather bulletins and once they were on the notebook I could access them at any time. Likewise, I had hard copies from the Furuno. These had to be kept dry as if they get wet they are useless, and if you try to dry them close to a fire source they turn Black!

MailASail and its facilities require a satellite phone. Initially, in 2012, I used my Iridium solely for voice contact. I relied on its own stubby antenna, from the cockpit, if and when the weather was not helpful, after 20 minutes I would give up for the day, and hope for better, the next day. It was not an ideal set up. I found an electronic engineer and asked if he could make me a suitable cable for an outside rail mounted aerial. He had to wait for some parts from abroad and I ended up with a 7-metre cable. This was perfect for my set up. Thereafter weather did not interfere with my satellite connection.

Navtex…this was fine in the channel and off France, but I did not get anything further afield. The unit I bought in 2007 is still on board, but hardly gets used.

Chapter 3
Jester Azores Challenge 2012

Panta Rhei means everything flows in ancient Greek. It follows a saying of Heraclitus; a Greek philosopher: "No man ever steps in the same river twice, for it's not the same river and he's not the same man."

This is my favourite saying philosophy. I am quite aware that the gale eventually will come and that it will pass. Nothing lasts forever. Even Bill ascribes to that. When I was discussing tactics with Bill in Plymouth he mentioned to me about slicks and that the gales are short lived in summer. When I mentioned to him about Denis' 7-day stint in a gale, Bill's reply was that Denis had gone too far north, stay further south and you will be fine.

Roger Taylor gave an evening lecture at our club in Gosport in February or March 2012 about his solo adventures and I took Jackie along. Roger at his introduction acknowledged me as his friend. We had met at the Jester do in London. I thought for a minute that he would mention my participation in the forthcoming JAC. I had not disclosed at that time of my plans to take part in the Challenge to Jackie. This came some time later while having lunch, she was surprised but understanding.

Jackie was busy on the day of my departure, so I drove down to the boat, loaded everything and drove back home, Eventually, taking the bus to go to the boat. I sailed off and went via NCSC to drop off my dinghy. Paul and Danny came out to pick it up. Danny took some photos which I have not seen to this day. I cleared the Needles in the same tide and set sail for Plymouth. I had not used the Hasler self-steering before but as the weather was fine I used my Raymarine 1000 auto pilot. That worked well until the next morning when I could hear some strange noises up above. The mounting I had fixed in the cockpit for the auto pilot had come adrift. There was not much wind, so I had to hand steer into Plymouth.

I stopped for fuel and the guy there told me to moor in the Jester designated area next to a psychedelically painted boat. That was

Nigel's 30-foot kingfisher. There were a few Jester boats about. More came, like Denis tying outside of me, with John on board when they started to bombard me with their questions, after the third one when they asked whether I was rich and the reply was negative, I went on the offensive and asked them what is the next question. That put a stop to the interrogation. Weeks later in Horta, John said that he simply wanted to be friendly.

There were presentations and a meal. I made enquiries about a carpenter and a rigger. The auto pilot fixing had to be mended and the wind instrument on top of the mast had worked loose. Bill volunteered to fix them both. I got some scrap teak from the marina carpenter and the job was done. Bill would not accept any payment whatsoever. Then a Polish guy turned up with his boat on a trailer, which started leaking when launched. They found some very dodgy things on his boat, however, Bill together with Roger Taylor had a go at fixing them…they spent quite some time. The fuelling arrangements on the boat were not up to scratch but they left those alone.

Everything was alien to me, I recognised very few faces, there were quite a few wives and friends. Nigel used to invite me around for coffee and drinks, Spiced Rum was his tipple. He had a dozen special glasses, his boat was very spacious and well-adapted for solo sailing, this was not his first crack at things. He had the same self-steering and when I asked how he does things, he said I would find out myself once we were out.

We cast off and started the challenge, it was foggy and one of the cross-channel ferries was due in. I noticed that John was tactically aware of the tack he had to take. The others went the other way. I went John's way but when I tacked I was heading straight for the ferry. Denis shouted a warning and I turned back on time. One life down.

I chose to go south rather than west, I got tangled up in the shipping lane, and had an encounter with a rusty banana boat which played cat and mouse with me. When I asked him why he changed course, he told me that he wanted to give me some wind room, and not block my wind. I could see all the rust on his side.

Winds were predominantly from SW, so I could not lay the course straight for Terceira. Tack and re-tack all the way. Encountered my first gale and went to survival mode, minimal headsail and three reefs in the main. I would take the waves on the bow quarters, depending on the tack. The gale lasted a day and it took another 3 days for the waves to subside. The wind direction may change but who is to tell the waves to change too? So, you get confused seas. You make little progress as the waves continue to hit you from all over the place. The course suffers.

Had an encounter with the whales one early morning, I could see this sperm whale very close on my star board side, started moving towards me, her eye looking at me, and me looking straight into her eye and me saying, *"What a way to die."* She dived only a few meters away from me, diagonally passing right under the cockpit. But she did not touch me. Surfaced further on and joined the others and they all left. What a scary moment. I had a long way to reach land, rescue would have taken many hours to come.

I soon got the hang of the self-steering and felt confident.

The Marlec developed a bad habit of wanting to unscrew itself. Eventually as I had no Loctite with me I taped the bolts with electrical insulating tape. I had to use the same technic with the bolts on the furling gear drum connection.

I had used plastic electrical cable ties to secure wiring on the pulpit and I scratched myself to bits. I replaced these ties by winding electrical insulation tape there too. The sun eventually bleaches this red tape to almost transparent.

The winds being again head on and persistently on the 6 to 7 Beaufort, one night I thought I would push the boat and left quite a bit more sail up than usual. Woke up in the morning about 5ish checked the sails and decided not to reef despite the fact that the wind was still piping. Few minutes later the boat almost stood upright. The headsail was torn to bits and the wind no longer helped much with the forward movement. So, I rolled in what was left of it. At daybreak, fixed the inner forestay in place and used one of the hank-on sails. I was on my knees and the green seas engulfed me a number of times. It was sunny and warm. I felt the briny water a number of times in my mouth.

I became an AIS anorak, anything that went on the screen I took it's details down, irrespective whether they were on collision course on not. In case, I was knocked down there should be some evidence as to my whereabouts. I had to prove somehow, I was there.

Then a few days later the fog set in. On the last Saturday, I saw a sailing boat go by, it had a massive head sail on, ghosting by. I was debilitated with a smaller head sail. Later from the arrival times I found out that it was Andy's Bula.

Sunday night to Monday morning, I was dreaming that I was sharing a berth with Larsen who kept on poking me in the ribs and disturbing my sleep. I woke up to tell him off…Went up on deck and I could see Terceira fully illuminated. The whole eastern side of the island was ablaze in light. 23 NM to go, and the time 03.15…I thought of slowing the boat down, by now we were on a run, after a number of idle days.

By daylight, I could see some local fishing boats around. Some dolphins came around to play with my self-steering blade. I had read that sometimes they attack the blades. As I was thinking of getting the hook and scare them off they moved away on their own accord. Were they able to read my mind?

One night, probably half way across accidentally, I stepped on the ignition key. It did not break totally and somehow, I managed to get it out of the ignition. But I had no spare key on board, so I was without engine and possibly reduced electric power. I was thinking of asking Jackie to send me the spare key I kept at home. As I was approaching Vitoria I called the Marina Office, the Pilots and the Coast Guards but I had no response. Then all of a sudden, I heard some conversation going on among our Jester guys. I saw one yacht leaving harbour and going north and then another going south. I waited for a gap in their conversation and butted in. It was Roger and I told him of my predicament, no key no engine. He said he would come and tow me into the marina. The wind started to die down and my progress was now slow. Roger in his Ella Trout III with Tony on board came and waited for me to cross the line and then took me in tow. I was given the space Fly was in. The marina was full. John Apps volunteered to fix my ignition by fitting two switches in place of the key start.

I told them of the hallucinations I had during the trip and that no one had mentioned them in the past so at least I was aware of them. Thomas said that he had them too. Now I know that most of them get them. Why did I have to be the first person to mention them? Is it taboo to talk about it?

I was the eleventh to arrive out of 29 that left I believe. Andy had arrived the night before, so it was Bula that overtook me. When I told them that I lost my headsail because I pushed for speed, John took me to John M's boat that had lost the mast above the crosstrees, about 150NM from Vitoria. When I asked how he managed to get in I was told that he had used his engine. In my racing circles that is not the done thing, jury rig will be the order of the day. But how do you sail against the prevailing wind with a jury rig? Simply wait.

We went out for a meal on my first night but I was too tired to stay for long. I bid them good night and left. Howard and his wife had joined us as well as a number of other skippers. Denis, John M,

Andy and another had hired a car and were touring the island, so I did not see them on the first day.

The following evening Kenyan Tim came in and he could not believe that I had beaten him.

Nigel came a bit later in the week. His catch phrase about his boat is, "She goes over one wave and then through the next one." Apparently, his boat is very heavy, 10 tons.

I asked Paolo, the marina manager, for a sail maker. Apparently, there is no sailmaker in Terceira just a man with a sewing machine. He has no spare cloth, no patches, no nothing. Eventually, I agreed that he could cut off the lower panel and get rid of all the sacrificial UV protective material. Just keep the leech line, I agreed to the price he put forward of 80 euro. He dropped the sail couple of days later, but I did not see him again. On my last Saturday I went to see Paolo and sort out the Marina fees. Paolo phoned the sailmaker while I was in the office and this time the gent asked for more. I explained that it was an agreed price he gave me, why the higher rate now? I could have left without paying anyway. There was a lot of conversation between Paolo and man, who accepted at the end the agreed figure.

There was an old boy in the marina who just sailed around the world but he found out that his binnacle was on its last leg and needed a replacement. I needed a better arrangement on my tiller for the fixing of the chain for the self-steering. The old boy arranged for us to be taken to this huge machine shop out in the sticks somewhere in the mountains. For 12 euros I think I had the thing manufactured and welded on the spot. The taxi fare was more expensive than the fixing. The old boy had to go back a number of times for measurements and fixings.

The next thing I needed to do was to improve the adjustment wheel on the Hasler. I found a kitchen manufacturing unit from where I obtained some 3 mm thick scrap door ply. The gent cut it for me to size, drilled it in a fashion, and gave me some more bits to hold my cutlery in place behind the cooker. I used Roger's drill for the job, tapped for bolts to hold it in place. Success. Also adjusted the fixings for the inner forestay by having to drill part of the mast base retainer and put a D shackle to hold a block. I went to the chandlery and obtained a jammer which I fitted with some jubilee clips to the pushpit so that when I lifted the steering blade I could jam it in the up position. Not easy this with the Hasler, as it sticks out almost the full length.

Dr Denis with his wife were there and they made him honorary Jester Challenger which he liked. He was coming back from the ARC with a stopover in Praia. He was planning to stay for a while in Praia and come and pick his boat later. One of his fellow participants was sunk by a whale and he was very sympathetic at my encounter. I met him again in Praia in 2016 and again in 2017. I consulted him about my bad knee and put me at ease and said that I should check it up back in UK.

Gradually skippers started to leave. Denis followed John M as a precaution to Horta. John was to leave his boat in Horta for a year. Apparently, a replacement mast would take 3 months to arrive, so the boat is to be collected the following year. Then Tony Head left and on Saturday, John Apps left when I went on an island tour. On Monday, I took the ferry and went to stay for 4 nights in Pico. The ferry called at Graciosa, then at Velas, in Sao Jorge and across the water to Pico. An excellent break from sailing and the confines of my boat. I undertook a number of trips including one to Horta where I met John who put me on a bus to do the island tour, after we had breakfast on a French boat and a drink at Peter's Café Sport and cake at another establishment.

The ferry was, Santorini Express, with Greek crew. It was very strange to see the pilots getting on board to dock the ship. Simply to comply with regulations as the Greeks are very skilled in docking and leaving, they do this so fast in Greece that is almost unbelievable. I timed them with Jackie when we were 'island hopping', in 5 minutes docked, unloaded, reloaded and left.

In S Roque do Pico, where the ferry docks in Pico, I stayed in an old colonial monastery built from lava stones probably a metre or so thick. No Wi-Fi will transmit within the confines of the monastery, you had to go to a special room set aside for Wi Fi. Down the road the council provided free Wi Fi in the Museum. I mainly had my meals at the Clube Naval which is close to Museo Baleeira (Whale Factory turned into Museum). The factory ceased trading in 1984. Some of the machinery was built in England. Apparently, the village was dirty, the smell was terrible and people could not put their washing to dry because of the belching chimneys. Pity they did not allow photography in the museum. It was a period of national football games, Spain was playing Portugal and the Clube Naval was packed, you could find a chair but not necessarily a table. I ordered and then asked a young man whether I could share his table. He was alone, from Graciosa, and was camping at the other side of the village. His parents were teachers back in Graciosa, his English was good and thereafter we met for a chat during our evening meals. He was a mine of information, he was in love and he was suffering from a recent rejection, I became his confidant.

I returned back to Vitoria on Friday evening. The taxi driver asked me for 8 euro for the fare, I explained to him that from the marina to the docks was 7 euro but the return was 8, why? He accepted my 7 euro.

When I reached JABA, Trevor invited me on board Jester for a drink, later Howard joined us on Jester for a chat, I left for an early night. On Sandpiper next day, Howard and I had a look at the weather forecasts for our departure on Sunday.

Dave from Wales in his Achilles came over from Ponta Delgada. Apparently, his wife flew in to Vitoria but as he could not head for Praia da Vitoria he decided to go to San Miguel. His wife joined him and after a week he sailed solo to Praia and his wife took the ferry, a Greek catamaran that plies its trade on the eastern part of the archipelago.

I left, as planned, on Sunday, but Howard went to Horta first and then lost the wind and drifted for days. My return trip back to Southampton took 15 days. All on port tack. Tony did it in 10 days to Plymouth, he had strong winds all the way, 120 NM a day for ten days.

Now a few gems from the log book entries.

From the Plymouth to the Azores log book entries, I can see now that the highest daily run was 98 NM and the lowest 21 NM. After 2 weeks the log stopped working so I kept the runs from the GPS. In those days I kept a page a day. There are entries there of my phone calls too, like to Danny while I was doing 7.5 kt.

There was water in the bilges, thinking that it must be coming from the stern gland I emptied the cockpit locker and attended the gland. This was not the culprit. It was not a matter of dipping your finger in the bilges and tasting it. Diesel does not taste great. I traced it to the water tank that had sprung a leak. Tightened all the connections, this did not cure it really. Over the years I had two Plastimo tanks split on me. They are fine in home waters but not on the Atlantic. My last and current one (Vetus) has internal buffers at the welded seams.

It appears that even on those days I had problems with the Marlec regulator and charging, there are a number of references in the log. I had even disconnected it all together. Strange looking back at these as the 504 was new and should not have given me grief.

How easily one forgets? Many references of reefs being put in, then shaken off etc. When the key broke I had 412 NM to go, the entry on that day has a comment, "I am really being challenged." 'AL ABDALY' passed within 6 NM and did not respond to my call.

The return leg log is a bit thinner, brown bits in drinking water, suitable for washing up only. Wind northerly for a time and steering 90 plus. I phoned Jackie a number of times. Had a shave and my face is burning, sun came out, the Windex and VHF aerial gone. According to Bill I had a bird strike. Set up the emergency aerial on the broom stick and secured it to the pushpit. I even phoned Mark to tell him about the engine stopper. I know he always wanted to save me money. I had a lot of trouble with a fishing boat, 'KSORA' which kept on switching off her AIS, then stating that she was aground, then appearing somewhere else, I first spotted her at 0300 hours and eventually cleared her at 0730 hours.

In the Channel I hit a big fish that had a huge dorsal fin, I had to get up on deck and check whether the rudder was OK. I saw the fish swimming away from my stern. Nothing to report.

The Hasler is very sensitive to speed and sail trim. Too much sail and it will go where it wants to go. Balance is the name of the game. Reduce the genoa and the speed drops, mind you the swell, waves and gusts don't help either. Maybe you need a long keel boat for directional stability. I banged my head on the winch handle.

On the last Saturday, the entry states that for the first time since we left the Azores we are on starboard tack. After Falmouth the land is covered in mist and cloud. Probably is raining in Plymouth. It is sunny where I am with a westerly breeze plus a bit of sea breeze too. I photographed ALORA against menacing skies, something for Mick to enjoy. AMANDINE too. 130NM to go.

I arrived late at night and could not pick up my dinghy from the mooring at NCSC, somebody had over secured it. So, I picked up a buoy and went to sleep. Brian called me in the morning and I told him about the dinghy. He rowed to JABA picked me up and the two of us tried to untie my dinghy from the mooring. I secured the boat and went ashore and after some chat Brian drove me home.

Chapter 4
Jester Challenge 2014

It took some time to prepare for this one to Newport Rhode Island. There was the 2013 to Baltimore preceding this for which Bill Churchouse came around to Portsmouth Offshore Group (POG) in winter to sort things out on top of the mast. I fitted a new RNLI type VHF antenna, an RTE, a Windex as well as a Tack Tick wireless wind instrument. Also, we swapped a couple of winches for self-tailing ones. A very useful February fit out thanks to Bill.

I knew that a gale was brewing and I hoped to be able to make it to Plymouth before it hit me, crossing Lyme Bay was fine though the wind had picked up. As I approached Start Point the gale hit me. It had moved faster than predicted. I thought I could still make it to Plymouth for the Baltimore start. No luck as I lost my self-steering. The wind vane was not communicating with the steering blade. The interconnecting stainless-steel part broke off and sunk. I thought the prudent thing to do was to go back, as the predicted gale's path was to go north thus it would be an easy sail back with the auto pilot. No luck again as the gale swung east and caught up with me as I passed Portland Bill. I took cover in Poole harbour. Even a couple of the Clipper boats that were sail training looked for shelter in Poole. By next morning everything was fine, they and I headed for the Solent.

Before the 2014 Challenge I made a trip down to Plymouth to spend a day with Tony to sort out the FURUNO weather fax. It was an eye-opening experience, though I left with a non-functioning machine. Eventually, I ended up with a patched up machine for the crossing to the States.

I contacted Ewen and asked for an introductory letter for the American Embassy in London. You need to go to the Embassy to obtain a visa in person if you are to enter USA other than by air or Cruise ship. That took some time and expense but it will last for 10 years.

I wired an electric bilge pump in the cockpit to an independent third battery and fixed a third solar panel to charge this battery, which also powers a second bilge pump located down below. I carried a further 2 solar panels still in their packaging in case any of the others get damaged.

I met Len at his club cum teaching centre in Southampton to get an idea about his bungee steering. Later I went to his launch and departure from Southampton. His boat is smaller than mine and do not forget that he is much taller than I am.

I left the following week heading for Plymouth. I did it in one go whereas Len took his time and stopped on the way. When I arrived by the water break in Plymouth I phoned Tony as arranged and he told me to carry on to Tamar River Sailing Club where he was waiting for me. I tied up at the pontoon for the night. It was past 2100 hours, so you could not order food at the local Pub, so Tony drove me to a take away, I bought some food and he took me back to the club. I had not slept the night before so I had the meal and a beer and put my head down while listening to music. Next morning, I had to leave the pontoon and move next to Len who was on a swinging mooring. I had not noticed him the night before. Tony took both of us down to Plymouth for shopping and drove us back to the Club. This time we had a meal at the local pub. We used Len's inflatable for getting ashore. I went down town by bus and the arrangement was that when I came back I would call him on the mobile and he would come and pick me up.

Paul's boat was the only one in QAB marina when I looked in. On Friday morning, we moved down there ourselves too. Andy and Howard joined us. Roger came a bit later. Of 40 boats on the list, it was only 5 of us that were there on the day. Though there were some more skippers around. Bill, Bob and Denis come to mind. Bob acted as our transport for our top up shopping. Tony invited us to his house for a drink, Norman and Guy were there too. Guy was still working on his boat and would not leave for quite some time yet. That was my second visit to Tony's house. (I from the Caribbean, Guy from Newport RI on our return journeys met in Terceira in 2017).

On Saturday night we went out for a meal, Paul, Howard and I, and Len paid for all of us from his shopping coupons. It was decided that we would not set off on Sunday as planned because there was a blow in the Channel. So, we technically had a start as the gun was fired, but we stayed put in our berths. Andy decided to move to Cawsands for the night.

I was having some teething problems with access to my MailASail email. I was fine from ashore but not from the boat. In the Azores in 2012, a British guy in the marina checked my sat phone, the cable and the modem and told me that I had the wrong modem which I replaced when I got back. So, what was the problem this time? Howard at the Royal Western Club checked my software and found nothing wrong with it. He suggested it might be the USB cable. I went into town and bought another one. Although the screw fittings were the opposite of what I needed, I dismantled the connector and took the screws off and secured the modem to the cable with electrical insulation tape. This setup worked and survives to this day. Howard did his magic again in the afternoon. Had we sailed as planned I wouldn't have had access to MailASail's blog facilities.

Monday 12th May, Bill came down in the morning to see us off and he let my lines off telling me to take it easy and go south. In Plymouth sound I met Len who had cast off only minutes before me. He took some pictures of me which he passed on to me after our return to UK.

I went for the Eddystone Light House, Len stayed close to land. Paul called on the VHF and I told him that we split. He said to keep in touch. We had not made arrangements before-hand and that was the last I heard from anyone.

There were some strong winds but for a change these northerlies helped me to reach the Azores in good time. On Saturday noon (24-5-2014) when I switched on my Iridium to call Jackie, there was a message for me to call the Coastguard in Falmouth. Why I thought? So far everything was fine. While I was still in Plymouth Jackie was preparing to fly to Spain with her Yoga class. I knew she was to return to UK on Saturday hence my switching on my sat phone. So, I phoned the coastguard and was told that none of my SPOT messages were received, last one received was on the 15th, and Jackie on the advice from someone on the net phoned the Coastguard. I reassured them that everything was fine and that I was NE of the Azores. They told me that they will get in touch and pass the message to Jackie. Later, I phoned Jackie and she told me some unknown person on the internet advised her to call Falmouth. I do not know why she panicked or why she took this person's advice? Later, it transpired that I had not set up my Spot account correctly, so I phoned Tony with my password etc. and he kindly reset my account and added a number of fresh names to the list of recipients.

Couple of days later early in the morning, I noticed that the self-steering gear looked crooked. On investigation I saw that one half of the bracket had sheared off and the other side split half way. It must have been the following strong winds that caused this. I was about 120 NM from Terceira, the wind was dead ahead. It was going to take a couple of days with all the tacking. Instead I decided to go for the eastern side of San Miguel, less tacking, but as the wind veered gradually, I aimed for the western end. Then the wind died. Now I was using the autopilot and I decided to bring the self-steering back on the boat. It took some time and a big effort. This was another huge item to store on the boat. Storage in a small boat is a big problem. However, I was saving some time and time was of the essence. While I was doing this between San Miguel and Terceira a number of whales took some interest and kept on circling the boat. When I stopped for a rest I noticed a gas smell, turned off everything pumped the bilges, the smell persisted, so disconnected the cylinder and everything and decided to have cold meals for a change, after all, I was now close enough to a port.

Now this bracket has its own story. Abbey Engineering did the original two brackets from mild steel, they were manufactured in pieces and welded together and fitted like a glove. They were not identical or interchangeable, as the transom of the boat had its own peculiarities. While two members in the club were towing a boat by tractor in the yard, the standing rigging of the tow caught my self-steering and bent the bracket. The guys were very apologetic. I took the self-steering off and tried to hammer the bracket back into shape. Hurt my finger in the process which took months to mend. After some discussion I decided to make the brackets in stainless-steel, but instead of sticking with the original engineer I opted for a cheaper option and asked a welder, to do the job. I gave him the brackets and the piece of wood on to which the self-steering would fit. When I put the assembly on the boat it would not fit. I called the welder around and he could see the problem, he had tried to bend the 5 mm stainless bar and the inside gap was too small. He was not prepared to do anything about it. His previous attempt at making a T-pole to mount the aerials on was too short and had to be modified. I decided to put some very thick stainless washers under the brackets and thus straddle the transom.

This arrangement worked but I had to insist on some additional triangular brackets for support, which in his version consisted of half an inch by two inches triangle, stating that it would be adequate. Unfortunately, not in the Atlantic! My mistake was to trust him, or for choosing a less knowledgeable tradesman and not an engineer.

When on my approach to Ponta Delgada I called the Marina on VHF the harbour master told me to go to the west marina and pick up a berth I fancied and then come and see him. The Greek catamaran ferry was in port. The marina office is split in two, in the new western part you have all the facilities, laundry, showers etc. and the polyglot helpful Isabel in the office. The other office is in the old marina where the fuel, customs, police, immigration etc. are based.

In this old part a German couple were trading as repairs and chandlery. They live on board their yacht in the marina. Tom came to help with the dismantling of the bracket remnants from the transom and liaise with local engineer to make a replacement bracket to my specifications. It cost 100 euro to Tom and in turn he charged me 120 euro. He tried to fix the leaking water tank by adding some sticky material at the fittings. His hourly labour charge was 35 euros. Cash in hand jobs only, his only trade is with visitors, the locals have friends who have friends.

I spent some time in sourcing a hose and a new regulator for the gas. The hose available in the Azores is 8 bar and very stiff, took me ages to secure it. As I had no connection to gas I could not heat water to soften it. Do I need a spare gas canister and cooker for emergencies? I also had a new ignition key cut as I managed to bend the original key. Now I go without a key in the ignition!

The repairs and provisioning took three days, when I left Ponta Delgada there was hardly any wind. I struggled for days to make any headway, lovely sunny days but hardly any wind, worse at nights as the light breeze disappears altogether.

Fresh milk does not last more than two days without a refrigerator. As they do not do half litre cartons most of the milk bought went over the side.

Northwood predicted significant winds to our north, they hit us at 28kt to start with then went up to 32kt zero viz and rain. The anode wire terminal for a second time had to be fixed to the rudder stock. Despite the winds I had my shave and wash.

One important job I do before I settle for the night, I put the nav lights on, not because someone is going to see them but to avoid a bird strike. Bill had a strike on his rigging and apparently it makes a hell of a noise.

Week 5 into the trip, I am on the other side of the folded Admiralty Chart. I no longer see Europe behind me but America in front of me. The winds are still head on, my westing is minimal, I might be sailing fast or slow but always not towards my destination, the VMG (velocity made good) is very poor. All this is adding to the days at sea. I had lost a lot of time in the light winds and now the head winds are not helping much.

My blog from that time recalls the three 'T' shirt stories. In fact, turned out to be four 'T' shirts.

In 1996 I went on a guided Orchid Tour of Thailand, where I bought a T shirt at the International Orchid Festival that was taking place in Chiang Mai. In those days, I was mad about orchids.

The next shirt was a yellow fake CK one Jackie bought for me while holidaying in Turkey with Linda. Fakes there, are big business. (1997)

The third one was the one my son gave me after the filming of '1492' in Costa Rica (1992), 500 years anniversary of Columbus' discovery, with Ridley Scott, Gerard Depardieu, Sigourney Weaver etc. John, my son, was in Pinta. In fact, he was wearing a similar shirt at the festival of sail in Brest I believe, in France when he went there with a square rigger and a lady took a fancy to it and bought it off him while he was wearing it. So, he had to ask for another one from the boat. It was this shirt that he gave me.

These shirts along with others were hanging on the line to dry, there were used on the boat as rugs by now, mopping the floor etc. When the weather picked up they all disappeared over the side. However, one morning while mopping the floor, I found the Columbus one tucked away. The one lost then must have been the one I made back in 2004 when the Greek Football team won the European Cup. I had that made myself and had a tiger head on it.

COMING BACK

On Friday 13th June, when I went on deck in the morning at about 0815 hours (BST) I noticed that the wind vane was at a strange angle. It was in its strengthened new bracket but it was not working. It looked as if someone had taken it apart and assembled it incorrectly. It had broken and needed drastic action to fix it. The seas were rough, I was on a beat. I disconnected the lines from the tiller, the autopilot could not cope in these conditions. I calculated distance to go, VMG for the past week etc. and came to the conclusion that it was going to take me too long to get to Newport without self-steering. I remembered John going without proper sleep for seven days in his approach to Newport, and he is younger than me. Taking everything in consideration I decided to go back. Turned around and then tried both Len's bungies system, and also Ming Ming's whipstaff system, for short periods both were fine. They needed attention to set up. I thought it would be impossible to fix the Hasler (self-steering) under the circumstances, however, after the wind dropped a bit I decided to have a go, after all it was human beings that made it so I could disassemble it and reassemble it with a bit of luck. I tied with light lines all the parts I was to take apart and hung myself outside the stern of the boat. It was a bit of a squeeze. I did not drop or lose anything and managed to reassemble it. Had to improvise a Spanish windlass to squeeze the metal parts together and also hang at the back and stand on the items that needed to be straightened. I succeeded and set course towards the Azores.

The statistics read as 1210NM from Plymouth to the Azores (Ponta Delgada). Azores to date, the return point, 775NM in 13 days. Approximately another 1400NM to Newport, Rhode Island. From my current position it would take me at least a month to get back home, 2000NM as the crow flies, if I am lucky. My food and water supplies were fine. Nearer the Azores I could re-evaluate my position and then decided whether to stop or not.

The batteries were down and the manual cockpit bilge pump broke down. I had to change batteries in order to start the engine and then dismantle the bilge pump and repair it with jubilee clips and by drilling and securing parts with sizing wire. I was kept really busy. A few days later, I thought I caught a cold as I had chest pains. I had no cough, no running nose, I could not explain it. When I stripped to have a wash, I noticed that my whole chest was yellow and blue. While I was repairing the self-steering, my chest was bouncing constantly on the top of the transom, hence all those bruises. On board I had my wife's homeopathic remedies kept away from electronics and I dosed myself on these (Arnica) and felt better after a while.

I read three books and probably surprised my wife by doing so. I do not read books at home, only magazines. The only place I read books is on the boat and sometimes when we are on holidays abroad. When it gets dark I put an audio book on but it is difficult to concentrate if the wind is up and I get bashed about. Bob got me a selection of 11 CDs with approximately 11000 titles. All read by Americans, as they are free. Some rain clouds to the north of me this morning and I am playing cat and mouse to avoid catching a downpour.

On the afternoon of my first day coming back, VENICE, a tanker was sailing west. I had my RTE on, then as I picked him up on the AIS alarm, I switched on my AIS transponder and the VHF radio. To my surprise he called me on the VHF and enquired about my well-being and whether I needed any help or assistance. That really surprised me, we had a little chat and I thanked him profusely. His MMSI was 538002060. I checked on Find Ship App when I returned back home and found that 'Venice' was registered in

Marshall Islands. This never happened to me before or since. Normally it is me who instigates the call either for a weather forecast or at what distance he picked me up.

Of importance is the fact that the self-steering is working fine though we have not been tested yet in poor weather. Jackie wants me to post the blogs so that she knows I'm OK. She likes them though most of the terminology goes over her head.

Food plays quite a big part during the journey as it acts as a morale booster as well. In order to conserve water, I use the liquid that the tinned greens come in and use it in cooking, so I end up with green rice. For the pasta, I use sea water in part too. There is quite a waste of water in an open pan. I progressed to pressure cooker after Denis' insistence, so I now use only enough water in the pressure cooker and there is no waste. I had to experiment to find the right proportions. Sunday's supper consisted of rice cooked with coconut milk, this gave the rice a silky finish. Half way through I added baby carrots. Chicken tikka masala was the meat part and for afters I had pitted cherries in syrup. The left-over of the cherries I had the following morning with my cereal. At times I keep on adding tins and I end up with a five tin pot, all very nutritious.

I still have another few days of sailing to go before I reach Terceira. The journey continued to be eventful: I was awakened in the night by the alarm. Another ship in the vicinity (7.2 NM, SOG 13.4 kt) was heading straight for me: we were head on, on a collision course. I was still under sail so I changed my course by 30 degrees. Looking at the screen I could see that he had changed his COG by 9 degrees and I could now see his two steaming lights. I was safe. Out of interest I contacted him on the VHF to ask him when he picked me up on his radar – 7 NM, it was useful to know that my NASA AIS was as accurate as his system.

The next night, I slept very little as I was keeping watch on a yacht behind me doing a steady speed (varying between 5-6kt) and slowly catching up with me. Since I was doing 2kt in a 5 kt wind, I presumed he must have been motor-sailing on autopilot.

The following night the wind picked up and I had to get up a couple of times to roll the genoa in, as my speed had increased to over 7 kt. In the morning the wind had dropped. Soon after I had my breakfast I was sitting down below reading when I heard a sudden bang and the boat started to behave strangely. I went up to investigate, and to my horror the forestay had broken and the genoa was fully unfurled – only held by the furling line.

I put my lifejacket on and set the inner forestay so that the mast remained intact. Thankfully the wind was abaft. Dropped the genoa and secured it on deck. Just for the record I took a photo or two too. Well it is not a daily occurrence to lose one's forestay. The wind was not too bad and the seas were relatively amenable, and I was not on the wind and this helped, plus the fact that it was daylight and everything went well. Eventually, I folded the genoa as best as I could under the circumstances and took it down below. I put a hank on sail on the inner forestay and carried on. I changed my course to get closer to the Azores. Now, do I go to the Azores for repairs or do I carry on with the hank on sails on the inner forestay? Which island do I pick for this repair/replacement? If the inevitable happens and the mast comes down I hope it does not hit me on my head, this happened to a friend's wife who died. They were good family friends of ours, Belgians, he was the plant manager at Ford's in Southampton and when he returned to Newport (Belgium), they went out for a sail and this happened. I had sailed with him in his boat many times.

I sent an email to Mike my insurer to ask for advice. An email came back from a member of his staff advising that when I reached the Azores to go and see a Mr Sweet. I had no choice but to reply to that saying that there are 9 islands in Azores archipelago and that he had to be a bit more specific. Horta was the reply and I trust that he is a bit wiser now. I sent an email to Tony too, who said that an option would be to fix a forestay and sort out the furling gear upon my return to UK. The actual part that broke is the rod that links the forestay through the drum to the stem head. It is sheared just at the lower surface of the drum.

I played around with sails, I dropped the storm jib and put a slightly bigger working jib in its place. I had bigger ones on board but I stayed on the cautious side. I shook one of the main sail reefs too. I re-folded the genoa but still not as good a job as one would do on a pontoon, or even in the lounge at home.

I was just over 200NM SW of Horta and possibly I could do it in 3 days. It was during this sail I had a long visit from the spotted mid-Atlantic dolphins. They stayed with the boat for quite some time, very light airs on a beautiful sunny day. Also saw a speckled brown turtle, first time ever.

Eventually the wind dropped to nothing, a mirror sea and my choices reduced. I had no option but to put the engine on. There was no point in arriving in the dark or on a Sunday when everything would be closed. So, I timed myself to arrive on Monday morning under engine. On Sunday at dusk I spotted a yacht on the horizon, more or less on the same course as me and under engine as there was no wind, probably he had the same thoughts to arrive by daylight. I could not really ignore him and go down below, I had to keep an eye on him. Eventually, I put the radar on and angled it so that I could watch it from my bunk. Gradually he was gaining on me, he came as close as a mile and a quarter. By 9 o'clock in the morning, he had overtaken me. I tied behind him in Horta for the Customs. As my last port was Ponta Delgada my clearance took only minutes.

The skipper of a catamaran, a Brit from Gosport took my lines and commented about the two extremes of sailing. The huge cat in front of me was from Bahamas, a luxurious marvel with 8 on board and me a tiny slither of a boat with a single guy on board.

I was asked to moor at the end of a walkway alongside another single hander that was close to the repair shop. I called to see Duncan Sweet of MAYS, who said, "You took your time," obviously he was copied of the insurance emails. Well I had to nurse the mast back and took six days to arrive. He said that he was coming around shortly, so I could not go for a shower in case I missed him. The following day was a local saint's day. A Brit came around to see the solo skipper, me, and have a chat, and offered the services of all the Brits, "We are here to help" were his words. Apparently, he had self-steering problems and declined to have it attended to by Duncan as he was exorbitantly expensive. Instead he chose to have two crew members on board for the return journey. I was charged a hell of a lot of money, for a piece of stainless-steel that cost as per the accounts 100 euro. Duncan had not seen this make before. "Aren't you privileged now that you are to increase your knowledge at my expense?" I said. Not only that but they used my snap shackle during the winching which they ruined but I did not notice the damage until I came to use it during the 2016 challenge. I gave this to an engineering firm for repairs. While fixing the forestay Jeff spotted that one of my lowers started to part company and I opted for a replacement. It would have been a false economy to ignore such a thing. They did not have 5 mm stainless-steel wire, a replacement lower stay from mainland would take a week to arrive at a cost of 150 euro, for 190 euro I could have one of 6 mm tomorrow if done by them. Well my aim now was to get back to UK as soon as possible, so although I chose the latter, still it was not delivered as promised. I was not really very happy, but there was very little I could do under the circumstances. Someone somewhere is always making a profit of somebody's misfortune. Though Duncan's service and expertise are second to none, let's hope everything stays in place as it should be.

Horta was packed and hot. I ate all my meals away from the boat. I provisioned during the day but I boiled my eggs for the crossing at mid-night as it is cooler then. The café was one of the suitable places where I would get Wi Fi too, as well as watch international football matches. I watched Chile-Holland, the Dutch contingent was very strong there, a lot of sailors around, the guys at the café did not want to watch the England game. I watched the Greek game and they won 2-1 and I was the only one that clapped at the end, all the others wanted the African team to win. While I was there I heard that Andy had decided to return to base too, and that he was somewhere in the Azores. I checked with the marina office but he had still not arrived. I left a note about my whereabouts. I left without seeing him and later was told that he arrived in Horta after my departure. Pity, we missed each other.

My sleep pattern was all over the place. I was up at the most strange of hours to attend to sails or shipping. This does not help with my hallucinations. Writing the blog is very time consuming as the boat goes from side to side and up and down and the keys I press are not always the ones I intended. Practically, every word is corrected as I have no stable platform. When I was on a cruise on Cunard's Queen Victoria I went to see how they put their shows on, talk to the stage manager and dancers. The strange thing was when and how they decide whether to put a performance or not. The dancer would take off, the boat moves up, they come down with a thump. It is the same with the keyboard here, but not as painful.

I left on Friday morning, the best course I could do was sail between Sao Jorge and Pico islands. I had a lovely sail but got becalmed by the time I reached the SE of Terceira. I was tempted to go to Terceira, instead I decided to wait for a bit of wind. We drifted until dusk. By morning I started reefing down, the wind had really picked up.

30th June 2014. Wall to wall grey and damp. Even down below everything felt damp. We were on a run during the night and now we are on a beat and still going south of east. Fickle winds kept me busy. I had a pain on my right-hand wrist and despite Voltarol tablets I noticed no improvement. Stopped these tablets and started on Jackie's remedies. I needed to stop the blogs as my air time was getting low. Jackie wanted me to write them as she wanted to know that I was OK and fully functional.

One morning while still dark I went on deck to check things and I saw this white light, thinking that it is the stern light of a yacht. I checked the AIS, nothing there. Glimpses of red were showing with the white light. I changed course, after a while I noticed the light was very steady and constant, it turned out to be a rising star. This is the second time this has happened to me on this voyage.

Some years back I went with Explore to Mali. I always wanted to see the Bandiagara Escarpment and visit Timbuktu. While at Djene we met Mike Palin. He was making the series SAHARA. We had a chat, took a picture of him on the quiet and when he looked around I pretended as if nothing had happened. Few years later, I was going to Himalayas and there he was him again with his series about Himalayas. Another few years later, I was in Brazil and he brings his Brazil series out. Who is reading whose mind? Coincidences? I met him also in Olympia one year, he had to brush pass me in his cream white silk shirt. The audience was mainly females. I did not stay to listen what he had to say.

It was not a pleasant day yesterday. I thought we would have light winds. Instead the baro kept on dropping and I kept on reducing sail, hence not a high day's run today. I checked the tricolour this morning and it was not on. It was fine last night when I switched it on. After breakfast I spent a couple of hours trying to fix it. I remember putting a new connector 4 or 5 years ago. It rotted away and the negative had come apart. I made some get me home repairs and hoped they would work.

Weeks pass ever so quickly, this is week 9. We had rain again this morning, have been going more north than east but this is to be remedied now as we are expecting north westerlies at some stage soon.

I find these ramblings very therapeutic, perhaps, that is why Jackie asked me to keep on writing. I forget all the problems of the day and week. Soon when we get to soundings I will have to curtail these as there is going to be a lot more shipping about, and my services will be needed on deck.

It was a hard day yesterday. A second French yacht approached from the port quarter, no MMSI, no bleep on the RTE, so I called them to make sure they had seen me. Husband a wife team on their way back to Britany. Apparently, there is a third French boat following them. Had a long chat with the skipper, he offered help with the weather etc. Good of them but I had my weather fax. Later they switched their AIS and I saw their number starting with 227… FLORES, I believe from Camaret.

After doing all the midday chores I went for a snooze, the alarm went, a fishing boat about 7NM away is going about his business, gyrating. So far, the best day in Biscay but the wind does not give me much northing. As long as I move I am thankful.

10th July. Soon we should be passing north of Odas Brittany. Yesterday, I was planning for the south of it. The wind backed up quite considerably. I am glad we are doing it at day time and don't have to be around in case there is wind shift again and we mount it. It would have been something.

11th July. What a lot of fun and games. I got up at 0100 hours and have been up all this time. For the record, just gone 11.15 BST. I had five fishing vessels to play with, then the wind picked up from 12 to 20kt. I could see it coming, quickly rolled the genoa and dashed down. Then we went over the continental shelf, what a strange area. I put the echo sounder and it was reading 5.5 metres, some churned up waters. The echo sounder by the way works. The depth now shows 165 metres. Cloud cover is 8/8, another grey day.

Yesterday I had Bouillabaisse soup with toasties, the latter I broke to pieces, excellent. Today I will have Moules Marinieres, I am keeping to the French theme, but both tins came from Denmark (Waitrose). When I provisioned for the trip I went to all different supermarkets, Asda, Sainsbury, Tesco, Morrison in Plymouth, Waitrose and the local Indian shops. Variety is the spice of life. I cannot have chicken korma everyday even though I like it very much. I was thinking of my dad this morning, he died 30 years ago.

12th July. I have been up since 02.30 UTC. We had a variety of ships, from cable laying to a strange looking one (I thought there were two trawlers from a distance).The first one was a head on collision situation. I think I had seen this one before, I need to check my papers sometime. I have just cleared that last MFV, for lunch I had pasta with herring fillets in tomato sauce and a beer. I need a rest. This will be the third night with reduced sleep. The time now is 17.00 UTC. I must go up there in case there is a yacht about. I did see two today and I did not pick them up on AIS.

I arrived at American Wharf on Monday the 15th at 2100 hours. Jackie came and picked me up. I took with me a few things including a tin of soup for supper. Went home had shower, had the soup and went to bed, the first time in a proper bed for quite a while.

JABA among Jester participants, Plymouth, 2012

Bill and Roger fixing Polish entrant's boat, towed to Plymouth overland, 2012

Roger Fitzgerald and Basil, Vitoria, 2012

Jester Azores Challenge 2012

Basil and John at Peter Café Sport in Horta, 2012

Howard and Basil in Vitoria, 2012

Briefing and Drinks on Black Velvet, from left, Andy, Norman, Basil, Len, Howard, Paul and Ewen, 2014

Only five entrants, Plymouth, 2014

Stopped in Ponta Delgada to fix broken self-steering bracket, 2014

Broken forestay, sail on deck, 2014

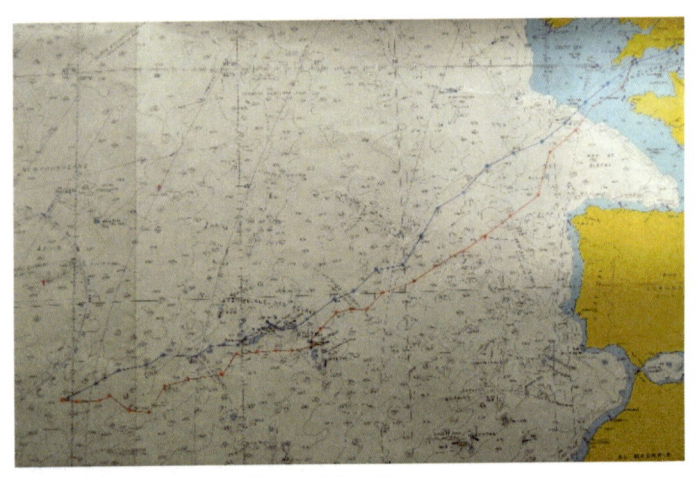

Chart of the 2014 trip

Jester Azores Challenge 2016, Vitoria

Chart of the trip from the UK to Azores, then Canaries, 2016

Funchal lunch with fellow French yachties, 2016

Lanzarote, JABA, 2016

Mindelo, Cape Verde, 2016

Storm damage to the reefing track

Lunch onboard in the calms

Mindelo from Monte Verde

Arrival at St Lucia, 2017

Soufriere, St Lucia, 2017

Antigua, Shirley Heights (English Harbour), Falmouth Harbour, 2017

Falmouth Harbour, Antigua, 2017

Wall Painting, Azores, 2017

Sunset

Sunset

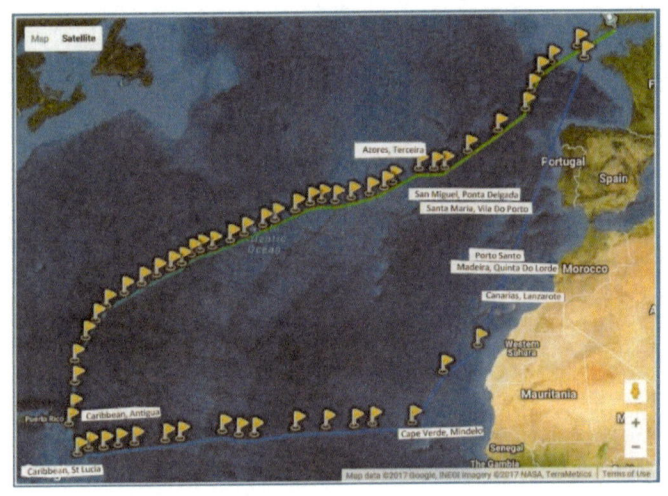

Chart of the Caribbean trip 2016–2017

Fastnet Race 1987

Hope and Glory, 1991

Chartered Maiden, 1995

Meet the Boat Show Team

With 6pm Sunday marking the beginning of break down it is appropriate to introduce the Operations team, all of whom would like to thank exhibitors for complying with the various new regulations and speed limits within the demonstration area.

From left to right - Dion Spiteri, Floor Manager; Mario Panatella, Floor Manager; Pete King, Floor Manager; Mark Crockford, Floor Manager; Murray Ellis, Director of Operations; Basil Panakis, Marina Manager; and Dan Taylor, Operations Manager.

Southampton Boat Show, currently only three of these still working at the show

Chapter 5
Jester Azores Challenge 2016

As you know by now I have had problems of some sort with my engine, mainly it was fuel starvation and at times charging. During 2015, Mick a fellow member of NCSC had a look at my engine and showed me how to bleed the system and everything looked fine, but my Morse control seized and had to be replaced. I launched and by the time I'd sailed up to Itchen the engine conked out. Mick came out to the boat in the marina on a rainy day and discovered a solid little black blob blocking the uptake pipe and advised me to take the tank out and have it cleaned at the end of the season and start afresh. I had already done this before the 2012 Jester Azores Challenge. So, the tank came off again cleaned and a draining tap was fitted. At the same time, I put a new Racor filter as well as a DE-BUG magnetic diesel filter inline after the Racor, an improvement used by all the Dutch fishing fleet. So, I was ready for the 2016 challenge. My launching day was delayed, so I only managed to launch on Friday and on the way to the American Wharf I noticed that although the engine was on I was not getting any propulsion. A small motorboat pushed and pulled me towards the pontoon and new problems started. The engine would not start no matter what combinations I tried. I phoned Graham who put me in touch with an engineer who was booked solid for the next 2 weeks. I phoned Mark who had done a number of jobs for me and I regarded him as a friend. He agreed to come for a couple of hours on Monday.

On Monday, I filled all my diesel containers with fresh diesel. Mark came on board and after two hours he failed to start the engine. He said that I needed a new engine, which he would have to order and he could fit it in about a month's time himself. He thought it could be the injectors, or the injector pump and as he had no workshop manuals it would be difficult to service the engine. He believed that the fuel was contaminated and disconnected the tank and drew diesel from my spare diesel container. I had filled the fuel tank with newly bought diesel only the week before and the tank was 7/8 full. After a while fuel started to come out of the tank's overflow pipe. It was at this time that he gave up and left. The arrangement was that he would look for an engine and phone back. I tried to phone him on Tuesday but he did not pick up the phone. Meanwhile I went on eBay and started bidding on nearly new engine but I was outbid. I even had lined up someone from Yanmar to fit it for me.

On Wednesday, I went down to R K Marine to have a chat with Dave, their service manager and told him my problem. His brain clicked the moment I mentioned to him the overflowing diesel. He said I should go back to the boat and use a pair of pliers and stop the back flow from the injector pump to the tank. He explained that he thought the pressure relief valve must have jammed and although fuel was getting to the injector pump, it was being redirected back to the tank instead of being sent to the injector. By restricting the flow, it would force the release of the relief valve. I went back to the boat and followed the instructions to the letter after reconnecting all hoses and pipes. The engine burst into life.

As I did not know what caused this, I made arrangements to haul the boat out and check whether there was anything wrapped around the prop and put extra burden to the engine.

I went down on Thursday and the sun was out and I could see that the prop was clear, so I cancelled the hauling out, and set sail for Plymouth. At the approaches to my club, Gerry came out and took the dinghy from me. Half way down Southampton Water the ignition light came on. I turned the engine off and started sailing but by Hamble the wind died down. I asked for a tow from a passing yacht but they declined. The breeze came up and I went as far into the shallows by Calshot spit as I safely could when the wind died down again. With the tide running out I did not fancy the idea of drying out there. I asked for a tow to Cowes from a passing boat which the husband and wife team obliged. Meanwhile I called the Cowes harbourmaster and told him of my alternator problem. I berthed at the outer pontoon and spent a rough night there because we had an overnight wind shift. In the morning the Pilot boat came around for a chat and they told me about Guy being down at Plymouth already. I was moved to Shepherds for repairs but nothing wrong was found with the alternator, while the engineer was there I asked him to change the water pump impeller too. Friday afternoon I left believing I could still make it for the start on Sunday. About an hour later I had the same problem, the ignition light came on. However, as the wind was fine I decided to carry on. I had a pleasant sail mainly hand steering as I was not that familiar yet with my new Wind Pilot. I lost the wind at Salcome and put the engine on. It worked for an hour or so and then cut out. I tried to sail into Plymouth. I phoned the marina to request being picked up outside the marina and also phoned Tony to say that I am on my way. The wind got lighter and lighter, the tide turned and there was not a chance of getting into Plymouth. When the engine cut out all the lights went off, no engine, no lights, no wind… Danger to myself and to all shipping. I called the marina for a tow, too far out, called the 'long room' they declined and their suggestion was to call the Coastguard, which I did. They in turn sent the RNLI to tow me into port. For a while the Coastguard was getting worried as they lost contact with me. I was on handheld VHF as I had no power on my main one. A huge lifeboat arrived and towed me at such a high speed that the self-steering blade lifted up.

Sunday morning, I went along to the spectator boat and watched the start. Afterwards I could not do much other than wait for Monday opening hours when Kevin the local electrician said yet again that there was nothing wrong with the alternator. I was prepared to buy a new one, but he said that it was not necessary. He fixed a lose wire by the instrument panel, as Bill had said the day before, and gave a clear bill of health. Tried to have my tricolour fixed but I was told that this was a two-man job and no staff were available. They were prepared to sell me a new unit to fit myself. Strangely enough this same unit was selling at half price at Ponta Delgada.

I crossed the start line just before three on Monday afternoon. There was wind and off I went. Approximately 24 hours late.

I remember Malcolm's videos when he used the say, "Oh what a night." I experienced that myself on my first Wednesday night, out of Plymouth. I had to keep putting reefs. The engine started by itself I stopped it, then half an hour later started again, when I stopped it this second time everything went black. No batteries, no electrics at all. I fell down in the cockpit and for a moment I thought I cracked my ribs. During the fall I bent the stainless-steel bar that holds the self-steering chain. A few inches more to the side and it would have penetrated my lungs. Well there is nothing anybody can do about cracked ribs and with no engine and no lights it would have been suicidal to return back to the channel in that state. So, the best choice at the time was to hide in the Atlantic and sort things out as I went along. I had a third battery under the sink, spare nav lights and in time I rigged these up. Meanwhile, I strapped a torch on the main which spread the light and hung another on the back stay. I also rigged my spare anchor light in the cockpit hanging from the backstay.

As I had no power to use the main chart plotter, I wired the 640 Garmin and RTE to the third battery. Wires were flying everywhere. I also rewired one of the solar panels to charge this third battery. I kept a minimal log of lat long every 6 hours, the wind varied and the baro yoyoed all the time. Wind shifts and rain, boat speed was low, at times I rolled in the genoa. It was not always gale force winds. I remember I stayed up all night and tried to get the best out of JABA, we were flying at a very good speed and direction, but by daybreak I was tired, so I reduced sail and went down below for a kip. By the afternoon, for the first time ever I could see horizontal spay flying around, whipped up by the wind, spindrift. The waves were not big but the wind was vicious, everything was white, thankfully this situation did not last long, probably, it was a cold front. At times I could do 330 degrees, but nowhere where I wanted to go. I changed the gas cylinder, life goes on despite the weather, eat, sleep, shave, wash etc. I could not do any blogs as I had no electric power, the spot (location equipment) had its own batteries so that was OK.

Vividly remember that I was in this gale that was taking me north, I donned all my wet gear, plus lifejacket and harness and went on deck to tack, despite numerous attempts I could not do it. It looked a lovely day and the rollers were huge and very well spread apart. 50 double storey houses could easily fit in the troughs. Went down below to consider my predicament and I went up again to tack no matter what, failed again. Finally, I rolled all the genoa in and at the top of the swell I managed to gybe the boat. I was elated as the boat started sailing south, anywhere other than Iceland!

I was nearing Terceira, ETA was going to be midnight to 0200 hours, the weather deteriorated, wind and rain, and I didn't think I could make port. I aimed to the north of the island and employed the parachute anchor, first time ever. All sails were taken down and the wind pilot blade positioned up. Drifted overnight and the following day until the front passed through. I lost 17 NM in as many hours. By midnight on the following day, I was 6 miles from Vitoria when the wind died yet again. RTE and AIS was wired to the third battery. By then all the nav lights and anchor light had perished in the gales. However, as long as the big ships could see me I was happy. I hoped the little boats would only make a small dent in the event of collision. I rolled in the genoa and aimed the boat away from the island. I thought I'd take a short kip and put the alarm for 30 minutes. I normally put the egg timer in a pan on my chest, this should make a sufficient racket to pull me out of the arms of Morpheus. I woke up 4 hours later. In that time, I drifted 2 miles away from the island. The wind showed signs of picking up, so I unrolled the genoa and tried to get a speed that would enable me to get into port in daylight. At about 2 miles out the wind dropped again and I started drifting. I called the harbour master and the pilots on the VHF and I got no response. I gave a general call and mentioned Jester skippers and Doug replied, who went and woke up Roger and Denis and all three came on Ella Trout III to tow me into the marina. By the time they reached me the wind had picked up a little and I crossed the line under my own steam. I had prepared the anchor to cover all eventualities.

Meanwhile back in Southampton, Len had picked up the AIS signal and emailed Roger stating that I was becalmed outside Vitoria harbour. Coming back from the restaurant, they looked for me but could see no one in the dark as I had no lights. In the morning, there was a fishing boat and a coaster just outside Vitoria harbour, in particular the coaster was pirouetting around me waiting for the pilots to take him in. Len in Southampton who has been following my AIS signals assumed that the coaster had hit me and was going around looking for the casualty, me!

There were six skippers with their boats in Vitoria out of the twenty that had crossed the line on that Sunday. I was the seventh arrival that had started a day late. The majority apparently returned back home before the first gale. One had gear failure, and another had injured himself some time before the start and had to call the RNLI to get him back into Falmouth. Another went to Spain. Of the ones in Vitoria five had decided to leave the next day, Julien for France, Roger, Doug and Denis for UK and Claude for Tenerife. I stayed behind as did Glen and Nancy, they were staying in a B&B as their yacht was out for repairs. Later on, Godot and much later Medusa turned up. I arrived on Thursday morning and left the following Saturday. Jester arrived after I left for Ponta Delgada.

Olaf was in the marina at the same time. He had decided now to build a house in Terceira instead of Flores, which he likes very much but getting there is not that easy. He drove me and Klaus to the ruins he bought and showed us around. Meanwhile I organised with a car electrician to have a look at my engine. But somehow, we managed to miss each other. He told me 1830 hours and he turned up early while I was having a beer at the café.

Sunday night to Monday morning all the lights on board came on and woke me up in the early hours of the morning. I could not believe it. I switched the chart plotter and it worked. I did not dare put the engine on at that forsaken hour. Denis, before he left, tried to start my engine but the ignition would not even click, he volunteered to stay behind and help me out but instead passed instructions to me as to what to do. In the morning I went on deck and danced a red Indian rain dance. Unbeknown to me I was spotted by Pedro who told me that I was doing a Voodoo dance. Whatever was wet dried out and good contacts were established. I started the engine and I was a happy bunny. The dance was obviously effective.

I went and found the electrician and new arrangements made. He came with a new battery for the engine. He found too much water and too many wires as well as some lose wires in the engine compartment's blocks. He knew which were the alternator wires at once. He cut part of the block and made some temp connections. Next evening, he came back after work and rewired a new block. He also prepared a watertight box with switches so that I can charge either the main batteries or the battery under the sink. He volunteered to make me an aluminium bracket for my cassette player but this item did not materialise. I still could not find my netting on board so visited the chandlery but at over double the price I did not bother to make a purchase. LED nav lights were not available here so I ended up with something small and weak, but better than nothing.

When Olivier arrived his boat had received a soaking, there was nothing dry on board. He had hallucinations too which he found very strange, mainly food oriented while he was in India. Tim arrived a few days later, he was a great company, ex-army officer, great sense of humour. I gave both a welcoming beer. There was another American lady skipper whom I guided down to the chandlery and then I took the bus back as she was entertaining her paying crew/guests.

I sent a letter to Len and told him about Olivier that was most impressed by his bungee steering. Olivier by leaving a week late he encountered only 3 gales as opposed to my 7.

Chapter 6
Atlantic Circuit – Jester Challenge Beyond

Well we have to start this circuit from somewhere, most yachts try to leave UK before September and head for the Gib, or the Canaries. They stay there until November to do the crossing. The ARC is an organised affair but there are a lot of others that do this independently. Also, some go via Cape Verde and this is the route I took.

So, I left Vitoria for Ponta Delgada, this was going to be my second visit to San Miguel. As usual I called the marina on my approach and he told me to pick my own berth and then report to the office. By coincidence I took the same berth I had in 2014. The police officer recognised me from last time. I called on Thomas and sorted the problem with the tricolour, which was due to a bad deck connection. Also, I replaced the starboard navigation light yet again. I bought some netting for the foredeck and a new LED anchor light. I thought it prudent to buy another battery, a Tudor, which came with a 25% discount. So instead of paying 255 euro, I paid 179 euro cash. Finally, I thought I deserved a bit of sightseeing so I went in a limousine with a couple for a day out, to the north and west part of the island, Sete Citates, Mosteiros, Ribeira Grande etc. Unfortunately, the day was misty and at times wet but the company and the trip was fine. Husband and wife were undertakers from the north of mainland Portugal.

Izabel the receptionist in the marina had phoned around and booked me that trip. Next day I thought I do something myself which would be less expensive, so on Friday I caught the bus and went to Furnas and its environs for the day. The botanical gardens, the Caldeiras, and also managed to get a taxi to take me to the lake, and wait for me whilst I took some photographs and a few general views with the camcorder. The locals and restaurants cook their meals in holes they dig into the hot thermals. The driver was a local guy who had recently returned from California, where he spent practically all his life. It was he who told me about the results of the

Brexit vote, fresh news of the day. Ten euros well spent. I had a burger and a beer plus coffee for 5.10 euro as recommended by an American lady in the café outside the Botanical Gardens. In town, some enterprising locals boil corn on the cob in these thermal geezers and flog them to the tourist a euro each. I had one and it tasted lovely.

Saturday, I left for Santa Maria. There was little wind but it picked up on the way. In hindsight I should have left much later in order to make an early morning approach to the island instead I had to reduce sail and slow the boat down. The port accommodates the ferry from San Miguel, the entrance to the inner harbour and marina is rather a narrow affair. The total population is 5000 inhabitants. Everything on Sunday is closed. There is a superb YHA hostel by the castle at the top of the hill. My Sunday walk was as if I had walked through a graveyard. Nothing was open. I had my meal at the Nautical Club in the marina. Smaller portions, higher prices than those charged in Terceira. I did not go to the club again.

Sunday evening, we had a light rain and as I was leaving the boat for a shower early morning my engine started by itself. For a minute I thought it was somebody else's engine and I considered it rather antisocial so early in the morning. However it was mine, so I stopped it and tried to find how it happened, as I had no problems for the past couple of weeks. When I opened the engine cover and took the drawer off I could see water dripping on the alternator and running over the starter motor. Using the torch, I saw a hole by the scuppers. Had my shower and then waited for the marina engineering shop to open. The owner said he would come around and have a look. The end result being, that they plugged the hole and also shortened the stainless-steel fitting on the tiller that nearly caused the piercing of my lungs.

My sightseeing in Santa Maria consisted of a bus trip to the airport, had a coffee and walked back. From the bus driver I found out about a bus tour around the island. So that is what I did the following day. Dave an ex delivery skipper, came around to tell me that he knew Denis and he invited me around to his boat, a Rustler 31, the original number one, belonging to Mr Rustler himself. We had some wine and chatted about what most sailors do. He keeps his yacht overwinter in Cowes and flies to USA to be with his wife for the rest of the year. He hired a moped and did the island tour that way. I have not done a trip like that since my solo extra trip to Samothraki, when I left my first wife and children in Thasos as they did not want to accompany me. That must have been sometime in the mid-'80s. I liked the take away food from the supermarket in Vila do Porto, it was excellent. I took some with me for the forthcoming passage to Porto Santo.

I checked the weather and the plan was to go first for **Porto Santo** and then to **Madeira**. A straight line of 500NM or so trip, on a broad reach, that would take five days or so. I left on Thursday 30th of June. First day's run was 92 NM followed by 106NM the next day. The AIS transponder showed RED, (error), the chart plotter turned itself off, the NASA AIS screen blank. Low battery again. I had to charge the batteries, so I put the engine on, it rained, but nothing untoward happened. No leaking. I was happy. I arrived in the marina at Porto Santo at 1700 hours BST. Couple of Germans helped me to moor in a rather big berth with the finger pontoons being as wobbly as the ones in Cherbourg. The following night I spent it in a much smaller berth squeezed next to a solo Frenchman who had built his own boat. He smoked a lot and the smell drifted to me in my boat.

I did the usual trips to town, I had a meal and did some shopping. I bought a salmon steak that just about managed to fit on my dinner plate. This was the first place that had introduced a charge for a shopping bag, so on the next shopping trip I came prepared with my own bags. My main object was to visit Columbus' house, or what they think could have been his house. Now of course it is a museum but prior to that was the priest's residence, the church being located next door. One Dutch galleon on its way to the Far East, was blown off course and sunk by the island. I had quite an interesting talk with the curator, as I could remember this story from my guided tour in Amsterdam and I relayed the information and in turn she translated to me all the Portuguese writing about the wreck and the findings displayed in the museum.

Leaving Porto Santo was an experience, the girls in the office were amazing. They managed to prolong the paperwork by chatting about their lives and everything under the sun with me. They were mature ladies that have never left the island. The credit machine being down did not help either. I can say they were very friendly. It was 0950 by the time I left the Marina.

Madeira

I put the genoa only with a light wind which gradually picked up. I had seen mountainous Madeira on my way to Porto Santo. The wind kept on rising on my approach to Ponta de Sao Laurenco so did the waves. It was still relatively deep but I encountered something like overfalls back home. Going around the corner the wind increased to 34kt dead on the nose, as I was aiming for Quinta Do Lorde. I could see smaller coasters going for Canical the next port along the coast. I could have gone for Funchal but for that I should have left Porto Santo much earlier. Len had mentioned that the scenery around Quinta is lovely and the Danish guy I met in Ponta Delgada had recommended this place too, as well as the Marina in Lanzarote, my next port of call. As I struggled, I called the marina, no reply, was it getting near closing time? Then the engine red light came on, it was overheating again. I called the marina again and asked for a tow in. A rib came out and on the way in the guy managed to wrap my rope around his prop. His colleague on the pontoon, instead of taking my line went to help him, so JABA mounted the rib. It was a comedy of errors.

The two German guys I met in Porto Santo were there and I got the internet connection details from them but I could not make a connection. The following day I took the laptop and the tablet to the office and the marina manager eventually sorted the problem by assigning me as a member of staff. That is how I got on the net. I enquired for a Volvo engineer to have a look at the engine. Joanna the receptionist did a good job in locating an engineer who asked for 80 euro to come from Funchal plus VAT, and his hourly rate was 40 euro per hour to have a look. No guarantee that he could fix it. I decided to try to sort it out myself.

Friday afternoon took a long walk along Sao Lourenco peninsula. Four hours walk in the wind, but it was excellent. The area was barren and parched. Saturday, I took the bus to Funchal, Boudicca, the cruise ship was coming in. I stopped at a café with ambience and had a meal. I left a tip and the waiter was most impressed, holidaymakers never left a thing. I enquired about a berth in the marina and was told that I could be accommodated as I was small enough to be squeezed in somewhere. One of the local sailing girls, as she was leaving the marina said that I would be better off where I was. Found a supermarket did some shopping and caught the 14.30 bus back. I changed my attire and tackled the overheating. I disconnected the inlet hose and put a long screwdriver down the skin fitting, no obstruction found, looked healthy as a lot of water entered the boat. Next, I tackled the hoses to the exhaust manifold. Took the thermostat housing off and found the thermostat bent out of shape. Cleaned up everything and reassembled the lot inserting a new thermostat from my spares box and replacing the jubilee clips too. This took about an hour and I saved a lot of dosh.

Len from UK suggested that I should descale the engine, so I went to look for de-scaler but I was met with blank faces. The local water is not hard, therefore no de-scaler is available in Madeira.

I made friends with a couple of French guys in a big steel boat. The owner of the yacht who had hired a car invited me to join them for a trip to Funchal. I had made a couple of trips there already, so I acted as their guide. He wanted to fix his glasses and something about iTunes. Then they wanted to eat somewhere but not too expensive. So, I took them for a little kerbside ambience. They had what I had the day before and I went for pork in tomato sauce with all the trimmings. It was just as good. They were pleased. Then we went up the hill to Monte and beyond. I had obtained a lot of information from the weekend marina receptionist regarding day trips, the best places to visit and walks in Madeira. So, I guided them up to Ribeiro Frio where we had coffee. Then drove through the mountains to Hippico, where Francois got out to see the horses etc. Apparently, he was from an old rich family but they lost their fortune. He suffered from depression and spent 4 years in hospital and now Louis is rehabilitating him, which is hard work. I know their whole life stories. Very interesting.

We stopped at Machico and I treated them to an ice cream by the beach. Back in the marina had something to eat and went to watch the final, European Cup finals. I knew France was going to lose…too much possession…same with the Germans… The Germans had played France and lost, the French played the Portuguese and lost.

The marina had been pressing Louis to move his boat so he came around and asked for my help. So, I obliged and all 16.5 tons of it was manhandled to a new spot. He was most appreciative, had coffee there afterwards. I was invited yet again for a beer too. Francois cooked some lovely dinner and I was offered a taster. I could taste the sugar in the sauce and I asked whether he had added any and he confirmed that he had. The yacht was lovely, they had proper arm chairs, cooker, freezer, etc. It looked more like a house rather than a boat. Louis was in Tahiti for a while living on the boat. He was a rich man while he was employed, now that he has retired his income had taken a dive. The boat would not really sail close to wind. The reason they ended up in Madeira was that they could not make it to Gibraltar from the Azores. How on earth were they going to make it this time? They had a hell of a lot of fuel on board, but even so. They were asking my opinion how to get to Gibraltar and beyond. He has been around the world and he is asking me! I suppose I do my sailing in a tiny boat and this counts.

While inspecting the boat I found that my starboard genoa car had split in two. Again, no replacement could be found in Madeira, there were other sizes but nothing that matched mine. When I mentioned it to Olivier, the French rigger in the marina, he made and fitted a Dyneema strop for me that lasted until Lanzarote, my next stop. This was gratis. I left for Lanzarote and three days sailing on port tack and the repair held well. On the approach to Lanzarote I had to gybe a few times in order to avoid the unlit Roque del Este. Quite clear on the chart but you had to go deep on the magnification on the chart plotter to pick it up. I do not sleep when I am so close to land.

I could not find a replacement genoa car in Lanzarote either. Used the impact driver I carry on board to shift the screws on the truck. I took the broken bits with me and flew back to UK to be with my wife. I bought a second-hand genoa car from The Barge in Hamble and Dave Poulter from the club modified it to fit. As a spare, I bought a new one which again Dave made to fit.

In July, the heat was really unbearable in Lanzarote and I was glad to leave, though Mel, the marina booking officer said it was lovely.

Lanzarote

My return was on Monday 14th November to sort out the boat, provision and leave. This time of the year the weather is lovely. Both engine batteries were flat and arrangements made through Christian, the Marina manager, for an engineer to come next day. The batteries needed charging, so he took them off and brought them back charged. Also, I asked for a diver to come and clean the hull. Christian the Marina manager was very helpful. I also collected the porta-potti toilet he bought and kept for me in the marina store.

Now that I had the engine running it was time to flush the engine. Chris, the ex-Cowes Harbour Master was passing by and we started chatting. He passed me the information about the boat berthed a few boats away from me that was draped with police tapes. Apparently, it belonged to a Brit who left with a Dutch guy and a female companion from southern Spain. Three left but only two arrived. The girl never made it to Lanzarote, she disappeared on the way. The Brit was in gaol in Lanzarote and the Dutch guy in gaol in Holland. There was more to the story, apparently the two guys had a speed boat and were running drugs from Morocco to Spain. Their sailing boat looked like a 30-footer in good nick, which would have suited me fine.

Christian had mentioned that the locals used Aqua Forte for flushing the engines, so I acquired 5 one litre bottles from him. It transpired that Christian's crew have never done this flushing procedure, so I did it myself with hoses provided by Chris. I used three litres and gave the rest to Chris. The procedure I used was that given to me by Dave, the RK Marine service manager in Bursledon. I disconnected one end of the uptake hose and put it in a bucket, then disconnected one end of the hose that goes into the exhaust manifold and put that one to the bucket too. The bucket had the Aqua Forte diluted with fresh water. I had warmed up the engine prior to this. Now started the engine, the water pump picked up water from the bucket and then discharged it into the bucket. I ran the engine for about 20 seconds and then stopped it. After 20 minutes did the same for another 20 seconds. I did not want to overheat the exhaust pipes without being cooled by the circulating water. Waited for a while and this time reconnected the hose that went to the exhaust. This way I used all the dilution from the bucket through the engine and out through the exhaust. Stopped the engine and reconnected the hose back to the skin fitting and run the engine for a while. A lot of crud was coming out. I could smell rotten eggs for a few days when I tried to run the engine. I thought of flushing the engine again during the passages but failed to do so. After my return to UK when Bill came around in November he did this with patio cleaner and in a different way. We warmed up the engine, poured the cleaner directly through the water filter, left it for an hour, and then run the engine. A lot of foaming water came out with presumably lime scale. The yacht was on the hard and we had to improvise our water feed from the mains.

Friday night in the Lanzarote marina was a disco night with the loud music not stopping before 0600 hours on Saturday morning. I asked to be moved and this time I picked my own berth out of the three choices offered to me. I berthed next to a Brit, Graham, who took my lines together with a French couple. The latter were fixing their heating on board as they were going to Patagonia. When I was looking for a quiet berth I asked Graham whether he could hear the disco noise from his berth, he said, "No," but his wife could, when I asked, "How?" He said that he takes his hearing aid off at night!

Fiona, an Australian, wanted to photograph a decal silhouette of an arty horse on one of the boats, not unlike that of the White Horse in Wiltshire. She wanted apparently a tattoo done of that design on her. She turned out to be the Captain of a 60 ft brand-new Lagoon catamaran on the maiden trip to BVI. Their brand-new engine blew up and now they were waiting for a replacement Volvo engine to be brought in and fitted. The charter for their Lagoon is £10,000 per week. I met her again one evening with her crew, names exchanged and I was invited on board. Something which I did not follow up.

Time was flying and I did not have much of a chance to see the island. I booked for a day trip to Teguise. Teguise is the old capital of Lanzarote and the venue of the Sunday market. Also known as 'La Villa' this town has a unique charm. Many of its buildings dating back to the 17th century display beautiful carvings in wood and stone around the doors and windows. I picked a Sunday visit and the place was packed. Teguise named after the last Princess of the native, pre-Spanish Guanche inhabitants. A visit to Cesar Manrique Museum followed. Cesar Manrique is regarded Lanzarote's most famous resident. His influence is so pervasive that it even incorporates the invisible. Thanks to Manrique there are no advertising hoardings scarring the island and high-rise buildings are banned. Even local homeowners are encouraged to get in on the act, by eschewing more colourful palettes for traditional white walls and green or blue woodwork, thus creating a pleasing, island-wide, aesthetic harmony.

Also, another afternoon I took the bus to Puerto del Carmen and these two trips were the extent of my exploration of the island.

I stayed next to Graham in his Amel for a while. We had a number of long chats: he takes his hat off (literally) to us Jester skippers. Apparently, he spent two years in bed with back problems and had watched all of Ming Ming's videos. He had also read all of Sandra Clayton's books too. I was invited on board his yacht for a drink and found out that his wife cooks Cordon Bleu dishes on board. That's why Graham does not lose any weight as opposed to me that I lose couple of stones every time I go to a lengthy sailing trip. Kevin in his Sigma 38 came around for a chat and asked about the two stainless-steel plates at JABA's aft quarters. These are the drogue anchoring points. Graham explained to him details about them and mentioned about one of his friends that was experiencing difficulties on a run. Once he had employed the drogue everything was fine. Then Kevin mentioned that I should not be leaving while the wind was in the mid-20s, stating that it was a bit too much for a small boat like mine. Graham looked at me and I looked back at Graham, but neither of us picked up on his comment. Tony was there too with his daughter fitting out his boat for the crossing. Chris passed a lot of gossip about the boats and the marina as he had been there for a while and was planning to stay another couple of years before venturing across the Atlantic. They had a wedding to attend in Cyprus too.

The ARC starts from Tenerife but the RORC contingent was based in Lanzarote while I was there. There are mainly two options for the trip to the Caribbean, you either go as direct as the wind permits you or go south to visit the Cape Verde islands, have a break and then aim west. The organisers of ARC now offer this option too. I chose the Cabo Verde route as the crossing becomes shorter, though the overall sailing distance and time is greater. When I left Lanzarote, the wind was in the 20s, a bigger yacht with full sail overtook me but in the interisland acceleration zone he was flattened. After 24 hours the wind died. I could see the Canaries for days, the passing ships told me to enjoy the weather as there was no forecast for the area. This lasted for four days. I could not really risk to motor into the unknown, my diesel range is limited and the distance to Cape Verde was in excess of 1000NM.

A pod of pilot whales passed my stern. At times there was a ripple or two and I started chasing the wind. The genoa suffered by scraping itself on the spreaders and eventually the stitching was undone. Sunday morning instead of being at church, I dropped the genoa and repaired the damage. A number of ships passed by, I must have been close to a shipping lane. I chose this as I did not want to be close to the African coast. Graham and Kevin were discussing about a friend who had electrified his yacht to repel boarders. Apparently fast ribs approach from Africa. Sandra Clayton mentions that they were shadowed one night by a boat that kept them on alert. So, I could put up with the inconvenience of passing shipping and staying awake during the night and thus avoid any piracy. It was during a quiet period in the afternoon when a water spout appeared from nowhere. I had been chasing clouds to get a bit of forward movement. Suddenly there was a dark cloud on my port side and I noticed this hose like connection from the cloud to the sea, it was moving towards me. I wanted to be involved and see what it felt like to be in it. I rolled the genoa in and stayed with a reefed main. I had the 'go pro' camera in hand instead of the proper camcorder so everything I videoed is distant. There was quite a noise associated with this water spout (hose) that was spiralling and extending from its cloud base. As it approached it changed direction just in front of me, instead of going to my port side went to starboard and after a while it fizzled out. Perhaps it extended too far from its base cloud. I envisaged items flying off the boat etc. and made sure nothing was loose and closed the hatch.

I have 12 hours of daylight and for 12 hours, I am in the dark, I read my books with the head torch on, I listen to music in the dark. With a torch I look at the compass and work out whether I am on course from reciprocals. I am surprised to find that many boats do not have this facility to read the compass from inside the boat.

The wind eventually picked up pushing me towards Cabo Verde. While I was on the move I caught a number of fish. The first fish I caught was a thin skinny thing with very fine sharp teeth, I threw it overboard. Next catch was bonito using a couple of meters of line, just put it in and tried to untangle the line when I caught the first one, threw the line in again in order to wind it in and the second one came along. I gave it a rest. I had all the fish I needed, it was lovely. A few days later I caught another. I used the pressure cooker and it worked fine. Then on another day I caught a mahi mahi. It was one meter long. There was blood everywhere, making a mess in the cockpit. The place looked like a slaughter house. I was eating it for two whole days. As I was pulling it in I could see another one by its side. Apparently, they go in pairs. I did not want another one, I could not cope with the pressure. I really felt bad about catching such a lovely fish. They have such iridescent colours, as if they were butterflies of the sea. They are of the dolphin family. Out of the water their colour fade very quickly. I lost a number of lures and lengths of line in between. There are some big fish around. Many times, I could see them taking a leap and splashing about. I bought the lures, the fishing line etc. in Lanzarote on the advice of Graham who showed me his fishing gear and the joy he was having in catching his dinner on his way down to the Canaries from back home, in UK. So, I invested in some gear and there I was lucky enough to catch some.

One night I looked back and saw a huge loom of light. It was not land based. Eventually the instruments showed that it was the cruise ship 'BERLIN'. I had a chat with the watch officer who passed me the weather forecast, the same for the next three days, it was blowing mid 20s by then. They were going to Mindelo. The instruments picked up another cruise ship the following night, but it was too far away for me to see.

Cape Verde

I could see Santo Antao, the most westerly of the Cape Verde islands, 60NM out as the sun was setting behind it. However, on my approach the following day it was misty and could hardly see any of the islands. The wind dropped and I put the engine on, then the wind picked up and at the interisland acceleration zone it increased even more so, I made it under sail. I wanted to make sure that I arrived during day time as their navigation lights are not reliable. The locals go and help themselves to the solar panels and/or batteries from the lighthouses. Len was telling me that the Norwegians had installed wind generators for the islanders but later refused the Norwegians to come and maintain them, so now they are disused. My Garmin chart plotter did not have the required coverage. The Navionics chart on my tablet was no good that far out. Close in I could see all the street names on the tablet. Instead I put a waypoint on the chart plotter and from the Lat Long I picked from the paper chart I navigated in. I had a look around for a suitable spot to drop the hook and then I noticed some movement on the fuelling pontoon and moored there. There is a terrible surge in the marina and to secure the boat I had all my lines doubled and some trebled. Even so one of my lines snapped.

Cape Verde is a group of volcanic island off the coast of Africa. An ex-Portuguese colony. There are 14 main islands making the shape of a horse shoe with its open part facing west. The western most island Santo Antao, is the most fertile one. Opposite this island is Sao Vicente where I stopped in Mindelo and the only island with a marina, but not the type of marinas we know back in UK. When Dave Rudling was here in 1992 he had to drop the hook as you still currently do in all the other islands in this archipelago. The capital is located in Santiago, one of the southern islands. Apparently, Cape Verde also suffers with immigration problems from neighbouring African states. One of the police officers I met was from Senegal, who was hinting for a bribe in kind, but I ignored the hint. The Americans regard these islands as the seeding ground of the hurricanes.

I stayed for about a week there, this is a third world country and you do get hassled. But the marina was safe, my boat remained unlocked all the time and I had no problems. However, outside the marina one guy wanted me to give him my T shirt, and the police in the Customs Office point blank asked me for money. I paid him the 5 euro he asked for the entrance clearance and later he asked for 5 euro during my exit clearance too. I told him that I had paid him last time. He did not press the issue and gave me my passport back.

On the first night the girl in the office did not want to restart her computer to book me in. So, I did not have a card to enable me to have a shower after 18 days at sea. One of the attendants to whom I was relaying this offered me his card and I had a cold shower. In the shower block I met Terry. I joined Terry and his partner Fiona for a meal. I had conch with fries and a beer and it was fine. I did not have any local currency and although Terry offered to take care of the money until the following day, the marina restaurant accepted my euros. Terry and Fiona are from the Isle of Man, their current boat is a Rival 38, SISU. They were on their way to Antigua to meet their friends who were there already. We had quite a few chats on board their boat, exchanged books and they joined me on a tour of the island by taxi that I organised while doing my walkabout. It was an excellent trip up Monte Verde, the view of Mindelo and the valleys were spectacular. Drove down to Salamansa where they do kite surfing on the beach. Then onwards to Baia, where the upper classes have their weekend retreats. Over to Calhau, a tiny place not so illustrious and then drove through the centre of the island back to Mindelo. There is some cultivation in this part, it resembles Morocco with its oasis. We picked the right day as the following day the winds picked up and we even lost our internet connection.

I was introduced by some French sailors to a café that had free Wi Fi and good meals. I had most of my meals there including cachupa as it is featured in Anne Hammick's *Atlantic Islands* pilot book. Cachupa is the national dish of Cape Verde, it uses highly seasoned meats in relatively small amounts together with grains and beans, and is slowly cooked to build a depth of flavour. Mine had a fried egg on top too. I had omelette with sea food, chicken, and Brazilian black beans (feijoada) that tasted better than the ones I had on my first day in Rio de Janeiro.

Tony and Liz in their Vancouver 38 came during the strong winds, with 8s and 9s all the way. Total contrast to the weather a few weeks back. I helped them out with their mooring twice, as a nasty American guy did not want them next to him as he feared damage to his boat. I had a beer with them and it was during that chat that I got to know them better than in Lanzarote.

I asked one of the local guys to scrape the hull which he did. Also, I asked another marina employee to fix my steaming light. He fixed it on day one and the light went out on day two. On day three he broke the fixing on the light and on day four tried to fix a new steaming light without success. Day five he wanted to rewire the boat! No way Jose! I gave him the light back and I accepted a bad deal. Len from England said why on earth do you bother with a steaming light in the middle of the Atlantic? He was right.

I used my newly acquired hair clippers and cleared the fluff from my neck. Also, I had a go around my ears. I will have another go tomorrow morning using the combs on the clipper this time. I remembered Tim giving me a trim in Praia with his clipper.

By Sunday I had had enough. Most skippers were planning to leave by Tuesday. Tony was staying a bit longer. The girl in the office was not in so I left without returning the plastic card that cost me 10 euro deposit. I thought I'd send it back with a letter to the German owner and complain about the office girl's service. When I asked her about the charges being weekly or daily, rates etc. her reply was that she put in the details of my boat I gave her and the computer came back with the charges. That is not what I wanted to hear really.

I left during lunch time on Sunday. The wind in the marina was 13kt, unrolled the genoa and aimed towards the south of Santo Antao. The wind started to pick up, broad reach at 20kt then 30kt and by the end of the acceleration zone to 35kt. Then, I ended up at the wind shadow of the island and had to employ the engine a couple of times in order to find some wind.

One of the large Martinique based French yacht that was moored in front of me in Mindelo overtook me a couple of days later. Never saw anything for miles. I had Christmas and New Year in the middle of the Atlantic 1000 NM from nowhere.

On boxing-day as Len had predicted the wind dropped down to 9kt. A smell of diesel had permeated the cabin. The day before I had rearranged the cockpit locker, as I was trying yet again to fix the alternator. The spare diesel container leaked and saturated a bag with ropes inside. When I mentioned the alternator problems to Terry he had said that my alternator is a bog standard one. In the morning I started the engine on the engine battery and the charge showed 13.5v. When I switched over to 1 plus 2 the charge dropped down. Checked all the connections and I believe that the water tight switch box the electrician made for me in Vitoria was no longer waterproof. The locker is saturated. While I was doing that the boat got pooped. I ended up sitting in 4 inches of water. This gave me the opportunity to have a wash (baby wipes) and change my underwear. I do not wear anything else, it is too hot. The alternator behaved fine on the way to Mindelo and at Mindelo, so I had no reason to pursue any repairs. I read the pilot books about facilities in Rodney Harbour, Martinique and Antigua. I hoped that the ARC contingent would have dispersed from Rodney Bay by now. The past two nights I have had terrible dreams about killings in USA and some other exotic place I had been previously. Someone is going around with a rifle all the time, someone I am supposed to know, but don't.

I kept the genoa for a week and then I thought to give it a rest. So, I put the main up and rolled the genoa in. I went like this for another week or so and then swapped again. Because I was so far south I had the wind always on my starboard quarter. I was getting weather updates from Len back in Southampton. I did not have much choice really to deviate. I was always moving, had a number of over 100NM day runs. Mid way across I changed my mind about Barbados. I wanted to get there for the simple reason that in November they had celebrated their 50 years of independence. It would be January when I would arrive, I no longer saw the relevance, so I decided to add a few degrees to my heading and go for St Lucia instead. I also re-evaluated my plans of whether to go to USA and do the ICW single handed. Here in the open sea there is no problem, I can cope. But holding the tiller for 10-12 hours a day, day in day out, in narrow channels, looked very daunting.

When it is wall to wall grey its nice and cool, the moment the sky clears to a bit of blue and the sun comes out it gets very, very hot. I have been watching the moon all the time, when it is overhead and the sky is clear it is like daylight. I videoed the moon early in the morning and it had a red tinge. There are now floating weeds everywhere, streaming along us. Sargasso? Is this what I am seeing during this last week? I thought of doing a bit of fishing but I caught a young booby instead, still in his brown feathers. Last time one of them tried to pick the lure, I pulled hard and he missed. I made noises to stop him trying again. I stopped fishing then. This morning a young one was already hooked. Initially I thought it was a big fish. I pulled the line in, I could not see the fine line let alone where he was hooked so I cut the line and he flew away. I gave up fishing.

I have not touched the Furuno SSB I have on board since 2014. South of the Canaries during the quiet days I hooked up the radio SSB to the Notebook but did not have any luck. I found it easier to ask passing shipping for weather forecasts.

I rejigged my plan of approach to St Lucia, plan A and plan B, in that I put waypoints for both the south of St Lucia and the north of St Lucia. Rodney Bay is close to NW of the island. It was a matter of approach, wind direction and timing. I anticipated to arrive between 1000 and 1200 hours. If I had come from the south, in the lee of the island the wind will be minimal and I would have to put the engine on. It would have taken much longer to reach Rodney Bay and it would have been an approach in the dark with many yachts anchored in the bay. The wind helped and I managed to approach from the north.

That last day of the crossing was the worst. One minute it was raining, then the wind would change direction. It was wall to wall grey skies. From the distance the first land I saw was the north of Martinique, a huge mountain that was covered in clouds within minutes of picking it up. It was the first time during the crossing I had to put my oilies on. St Lucia was low lying by comparison but eventually revealed herself. A number of yachts were going north. I contacted one British one and I asked whether there was room in the marina. He did not know. Some of them stay out in the bay most of the time with an occasional foray into port for provisioning.

St Lucia

Once I got around the corner and lost the wind I dropped the sails and the heatwave hit me. The sun was out and the place was in full colour. The sun was in my eyes I could hardy pick the entrance into the lagoon, I checked the waypoint and then the compass and went by the latter. I called the marina and had no response, nothing unusual I thought. A number of the berths I tried had 'reserved' signs hanging from them. I found a nice tight spot, secured the boat and went to book myself in. The 23 days on constant move took their toll on me, everything was moving. I missed the health authority and went straight for the custom/police office. I was in no state really to fill forms. The officer was most helpful and kept on telling me to fill each part separately. I was in the custom office within 15 minutes of arrival. When he asked how long I was going to stay I told him, "Until this office stops swaying."

When I called at the marina office I was asked whether I wanted water and electricity connection and as my response was positive I was asked to move my boat to a berth that had these facilities. The marina was built by Walcon. I moved JABA next to an Oyster 46 ketch, **Cherish**, owned by Peter Gray.

I took some photographs of JABA in the marina showing the St Lucia flag above the Q flag (yellow), when one of the ladies from another boat volunteered to take some photos of me and the boat too. Few minutes later there was a motion when a modern sports fishing boat came in with a huge blue marlin on the transom. They have a specially erected permanent rig ashore to haul and weigh the catches of the day. They were taking bets as to the weight of this monster of a fish, 500lbs to 600lbs. Apparently, they also had problems with their mobile electronic weighing machine. I thought that this will be a daily occurrence but I was proved wrong. This was the only time it happened while I was there. It was a magnificent fish, a shame that it was caught. It took two guys two and a half hours to subdue this fish. What a fighter he was.

On the other side of my berth was a Calypso Cat belonging to St James Club. Apparently, in UK they cancelled flights because of snow. The Balkans were hit quite badly too. The airport nearby is for inter-island flights. The international airport is one and a half hour away at the bottom of the island.

Later somehow, they managed to squeeze **Anakin**, a Comfortina 32, ARC participant too, belonging to a young couple from Belgium. I was invited on board for a beer in between their busy schedule. He is a renal surgeon in Brussels (Gregoire Assenmacher). He looked very young, much younger than my daughter who is a consultant of the same standing back in UK. Mind you Niki (my daughter) became a consultant some years back.

Pete was there alone as all his crew had already flown back to UK. He was to follow them shortly. They had joined the ARC and came direct to St Lucia. As one of the crew had a return flight already booked, they had no choice but to put the engine on when the wind died down in order to make it on time. I had a couple of drinks on the Oyster. Pete used to keep his boat in Port Hamble but now moved her to Mercury Marina, further up the Hamble. A lovely huge boat and now Pete is contemplating buying an even bigger one. This new one will have all electric winches etc., to make it easy for short-handed sailing.

Later on, Pete by email informed me that on his return he was to go up to Antigua pick up crew and go to race in BVI before shipping the boat back from Antigua to Southampton. Strangely as I was passing by Mercury Marina this summer after my return to UK, on the off chance, I thought I'd call in for a visit. The marina office staff asked whether I had an appointment and they refused to give me the berth number. Some call this security. I left a message in an envelope, and later Pete in his email said, "Keep in touch."

At Rodney Bay marina, Stuart, a Brit, was on his way to his boat and when he saw that I was on board JABA stopped for a chat. He had a 36 ft ketch, I cannot remember now whether it was a Bowman or a Rival. He was a lone sailor too, and we had a number of chats and non-alcoholic drinks on his boat. He was planning to sell his boat somewhere in Europe as the marina charges in UK are far too high. I told him that even if he wanted to give it to me for free I could not afford to keep it. On the other side of the pontoon from where Stuart was located was a brand-new Oyster 62 based in Guernsey. The owner was rather reclusive, though he had on board a partner with her two sons. Sam was young and very helpful, later on he volunteered to fix my lower stay by climbing Stuart's extending ladder. The nut that was holding the two lowers secure to the mast had undone itself. Sam applied some Loctite that Terry had given me back in Mindelo. Sam's brother an electronics graduate offered to fix my steaming light, but he had other commitments and he did not turn up.

My encounters with the marina traders did not live up to expectations despite all the eulogising of them in Chris Doyle guide books. I wanted to have my memory foam cushion recovered, the guy in the marina said bring it around so I can take measurements. As I was taking the cushion to his workshop, one of the local guys asked me if he can have it for keeps. It stayed at his workshop and heard nothing from him. Later he asked me to take it back as he could not fit it in his schedule. On my return back to St Lucia, I called again for something different yet again I got no joy. There is a Chinaman who specializes on stainless-steel fabrications. Called on him and he sent his assistant to have a look. I wanted the pulpit cut and a step incorporated in it. In Cape Verde and elsewhere they moor stern to or bow to. I cannot do stern to because of my self-steering. I will have to manage dropping the hook from the stern and motoring in. The pricing was exorbitant. Though the assistant was prepared to do it privately for a tenth of the price and also look after my boat while I was away. Never saw him again! I mentioned this to Stuart, who some years back had lost his rudder and they quoted him £1200 for a replacement one. Instead he bought two 8 x 4 plywood and some timber and did it himself for £60.

I called at the electricians and told them that I needed my steaming light fixed as well as adding another battery to the domestic bank. The guy who turned up told me that he does not go up the masts. He volunteered to do the battery. I paid for the fittings and he made two short battery leads and he told me how to put them all together. When I asked for his payment his reply was, "Whatever you think it is worth to you," that put me in a very difficult position. What is the going rate? Is it UK, Caribbean or third world pricing?

During both of my stays there, no guy turned up to fix my steaming light. They cannot be really that busy. Maybe they are choosy.

I took it upon myself to check some of the facilities and write ups listed in Chris Doyle's books. I bought 4 of his books in UK before I left, at £25 each. The Provisioning shop had a selection of goods but was providing these mainly for yachts with freezers on board, not for my size of boat. The grocery store did not have any tomatoes, so I went for a walk towards Gros Islet and opposite the petrol station was the bakery shop as described, a shack really, I bought some bread and a cake. I believe these were not baked in the premises, started talking to the lady about tomatoes and cooking in particular. There are tomatoes around in season, however she went in her garden at the back and she brought me one. I offered to pay for it but she refused to have any money for it. At the petrol station across the road I had a look to see what exactly they had in store, but there were only minimal supplies there. I think I bought a packet of cereal and a soft drink. Now had I turned right as I exited the marina I would have come across a proper supermarket. A bit further on from that there was an even bigger supermarket that sold take away meals too I only found these later. On one of my trips to the supermarket I struck a conversation with a local lady about some pork and herrings that were not refrigerated. They were preserved in salt, like salted cod. I had a chat with her how it was prepared and cooked and I decided to buy one packet of each. The herrings were really salty though you could eat them as you do with anchovies. Maybe you could incorporate some in the cooking to give a taste and seasoning. Somehow these got damp on the boat and I had to throw most of them away. I cooked the pork while I was sailing back to the Azores. It was a cheap cut, full of bones but tasty.

I had a number of take away meals from this supermarket and also did most of my provisioning from there. This was part of the Mall that had air conditioning and free Wi Fi. I took my laptop there and booked my flight to UK from there, on the recommendation of one of the girls in the marina office. I thought that a cool box is a necessity here, as I could not find one that worked on 12v I settled for an insulated one, bought a couple of ice packs and then added lager, cider, coke, milk and cheese. I even managed to save one piece of chicken for next day.

I took the local pick up bus and went to Castries, it was cruise ship day and got hassled a bit. I went to find out where the mini bus stations were, and in particular, the location of the mini bus station for the airport. There are a number of mini bus stations scattered around the town. I took some photographs and acquainted myself with the place. The town was buzzing, there were many old, interesting buildings that were well kept, the ones a bit further out, were somewhat dilapidated. I called at a creole cuisine restaurant and had a take-away meal. I ordered a small portion that took me two sittings to finish. American portion sizes by the look of it.

At 0830 hours every morning there is a weather forecast on VHF Channel 68 that goes for about 30 minutes. This is presented by a guy who lives in the marina on board his catamaran with his wife. All the yachts in the marina and in the Bay outside listen and contribute. He gives a very detailed forecast the like of which I have not heard before. Then he asks whether anybody needs to share a taxi to the airport or for a trip around the island. Yacht part exchanges are announced and he also gives a digest of news from home. I asked about taxi share to the airport but nobody else wanted to go the day I was due to depart. I went to his cat for a chat, apparently, he was looking for a person to replace him as he was taking his wife back to UK for an operation and they were going to be away for a couple of months.

Tony and Liz arrived and when Tony went to Customs they send him back and asked him to put his shirt on. They stick to etiquette. It was Tony's birthday and as I had been there for a few days I acted as a guide to the local eateries and we eventually settled for an Indian meal. It is such a pleasure to see Liz who is always smiling and she looks so happy in herself and happy to meet you. I called a number of times at their boat and had a guided tour of it. Tony told me to install a battery meter and lent me the manual to familiarize myself with its set up. The local guy said he will find something suitable for me but nothing happened. Then Tony told me that he had problems with his headsails. I remembered in Lanzarote when they were setting the twin headsail up and cranking the winch hard. I thought that they probably had overstretched the headsail and it went over the sheaves. Bringing the sail down a bit could cure it. By the time I went to see them they had taken the sails down and taken one of them to the sailmaker to shorten it by six inches. Three days later they got it back and it worked fine, "You saved us a fortune" was Tony's comment. The sailmaker charged him 300 dollars (local currency). They decided to sail south towards Grenada. I told them on their way back to call on Terceira. I left my email address and contact details but to date I have not heard anything from them. Tony was 78 and a couple of years before had a stroke and now he cannot look up towards the top of the mast.

They manage things by putting the engine on even when they want to tack. Their fuel tank holds 400 litres of diesel. I hope they are doing fine.

Peter left so did the Belgian. The catamaran skipper next door was very helpful and gave me some of his hull cleaning material and later he came around with four cans of beer, so we can drink to his health.

I made arrangements to leave the boat and fly back to UK. I thought it would be OK to leave the boat on a swinging mooring within the lagoon. I went to see the marina manager to ask for a discount, he is younger than me and very approachable. I asked for a discount from an ex-marina manager (me) to a fellow marina manager and the arrangement he offered me was really good, he treated me as if I were a local for my whole duration in St Lucia. The locals get preferential rates.

A Najad 36 arrived. The couple on board were flying back to Manchester and I shared their taxi to the airport. I had to spend a bit extra time at the airport as my flight did not leave until the evening.

If you are leaving a boat in St Lucia, there are a number of formalities that you have to follow. The deal is that you make a temporary importation of the boat and you have to list, in triplicate, everything in the boat (fixed or otherwise) and the lists get signed by the marina officials, customs and you. A customs officer has to come around and check this list. Can you imagine, it takes ages to prepare this list, and god knows how long it will take for the customs officer to check it. When the customs officer came around I invited him on board and to my surprise he checked the radar, the life raft and the wind generator and that was it. Otherwise it would have taken hours and hours. You have to pay for this service. But as I said it was not painful.

St Lucia, April 2017

Arrived just after lunch at the airport and had no intention of paying £75 for the taxi fare to the marina. I wanted to walk down to the local town of Vieux Fort and catch the mini bus but it was far too hot. I caught a taxi for 25 ECD which dropped me at the minibus station. 8 ECD is the fare to Castries and a further 8 ECD for my luggage. The minibus started making drops in Castries and he dropped me at the bus station for Gros Islet. The fare to the Marina was 5 ECD for me and my luggage. Total expenditure 46 ECD as supposed to 220 ECD by taxi. A lot of change left for Piton, the local lager.

It was hot, hotter than when I left, and it would get even hotter later on. I was not really happy at the state of affairs. On reflection I should not have gone back to UK in January, but stayed and travelled northwards when the weather was not as hot. Within days we had the Easter holidays and everything was slowing down. The day I picked to go to Soufriere was Good Friday. Castries was deserted, even the Cathedral was closed; eventually I found a restaurant in the market, ordered a take-away and returned back to the marina.

I fixed the battery meter and also the Marlec electronic charger. Tried the new screen Rene made for me (in Southampton) for the companion way. I had moored the boat, so the companion way faced the prevailing wind, this is better for keeping the boat cool and stop the prying eyes, but it was not much good during precipitation as the wind was driving all the rain in. The screen looked good and served its purpose, though it appeared a bit narrow. I bought another spare ten litre fuel can and filled it with local diesel.

On Easter Saturday I went back to Castries again which was buzzing this time. The minibus to Soufriere was not that far from where I had alighted. The minibus took the coastal route which is picturesque but very slow. Once you are in Soufriere there is a bus service to Vieux Fort. But this is a long way around if you want to get to the airport. The minibus service from Castries to Vieux Fort goes via the middle island spine and over to the east side which is more direct and much faster.

In Soufriere joined the locals for brunch and drink in a shack, took a number of photographs and managed to video some minutely clad local young dancers outside a pub like establishment. I waited quite some time for the minibus to fill and returned to Castries where I had lunch in a café that had stayed open. I selected what the locals call dolphin from the menu, which in fact is mahi mahi, I did not dare to have lunch in Soufriere as I did not want to risk missing the minibus. In this café there was a young girl accompanied by her boyfriend, who was a much older man. I mentioned this to one of the girls in the marina office who told me that the young girls prefer older man. I wonder, is it because of maturity or that the older ones are more affluent? The latter indubitably.

I did some provisioning and set myself to leave for Marin in Martinique. I started the engine and tried to move away but there was no propulsion. The engine ran smoothly in neutral but in gear there was no propulsion. Went to see Stuart and ask for some advice. An American skipper was there and they were planning to go for a walk. They both came around and the explanation offered was that I had something wrapped around my prop. We put a line from the top of the mast to the other side of the pontoon and I winched the boat so that it exposed its starboard side. The American guy, Terry, stripped down and lowered himself on a paddle board and with a spatula I gave him cleared the prop of barnacles. No rope, simply barnacles had encapsulated the prop. Terry could not feel the individual prop blades, a single mass of barnacles. He said that he cleared about 80% of this mess. I offered them some beer but Stuart declined. Terry enjoyed his, even though it was early in the morning.

I moved away and everything looked fine, by the time I reached the bay outside however the engine cut out. The wind had picked up by then, so I put the sails up and cleared the island. Much smaller local sailing boats were out racing towards Martinique. On the approach to Marin I put the engine on but after a while it cut out again. There was no way I was going to tack my way up the channel against the wind in the dark. So, the decision was made for me. I had to find a spot where I can sail in and drop the hook. I changed my course to sail up the west coast of Martinique. The radio was buzzing with French. The wind picked up in the dark. I reduced sail and carried on. The north end of Martinique looked really scary from what I could see. Everything was grey. Thereafter, the weather cleared and had a lovely passage.

I kept sailing as long as I had wind, Dominica looked brilliant. I listened to their radio and it was full of ads looking for engineers of one sort or another. They were asking for unbelievable qualifications. I wondered how people can get these qualifications living in a small island like that.

Guadalupe was very inviting, the wind was very fluky, I tried to stay some distance out to catch some wind. My wind was coming from NW and those inshore from NE. I passed the place where they film Death in Paradise, Deshaies, at 0230 hours, as the moon was rising. There were plenty of street lights around the coast, so the place is not really very isolated.

Antigua 17:00.9 N 61:46.8 W

By late afternoon I was close enough to Antigua, Monserrat was in the distance. The wind and the tide/current would not allow me to lay Falmouth Bay. I came as close as 4 NM but engine failure prevented me from getting in. I put a number of tacks and by midnight, I set sail more or less to SE and went down below for a kip, I overslept yet again. When I went up on deck, the wind had eased and veered, I could lay English Harbour with ease. To be on the safe side I aimed for the east corner of the island, I could always bear away if need be. I approached Falmouth Bay early in the morning, hardly anyone was coming out. Sailed in, headed into wind and dropped the hook. I was near the west part of the harbour very near a little outcrop of an island that had some brickwork on it. I was nearer the Catamaran Resort and marina, and close to the shoals. There was an aluminium Sarum 28 ft yacht from UK in front of me. A twin-masted steel boat from UK was next to me to port and also the Oyster 62 from St Lucia on my right. I did not manage to speak to any of these yachties. Called for a taxi service and got no reply, called to arrange a berth in the marina again no luck. I wanted a berth that I could come along side to. I inflated my own dinghy and rowed ashore, got wet on the way. I had my camera, passport, documents in a dry-bag. I was hoping that the dinghy would be there when I returned. No chain no special identifying marks, no nothing on it. Mind you no one had anything like my inflatable, all the tenders were proper ribs with outboards!

I had a soft drink from the marina and asked yet again for a berth. All were taken though some were empty. Simply their owners had gone sailing I was offered a bow to berth in the shallows but declined. I walked to English Harbour to clear Customs. A lot more complicated here, four five different sections after the initial computer registration. The lady officer was extremely helpful and guided me through. When she asked me for my ship registration document, I told her that it was on the boat and that I could bring it tomorrow. She would not have it. I offered her my passport in exchange for the registration document until the next day. I told her that it takes me an hour to row ashore, that would amount to four trips in a day, which might kill me! She was game, we had a lovely time, when I was going through the folder she noticed my insurance papers, which she had not asked to see. By going through the certificate, she saw the details of my registry number etc. So, I did not have to produce the document the next day. There was a super yacht skipper there (Jim Robinson) being attended to by a male officer in the next kiosk, all four of us formed a quartet and had a lovely chat. Jim had a pile of passports, those of all his passengers to clear. He remembered 'Coral Island' where my son was a deck hand. He was a deck hand on a sister ship more or less at the same time. He probably would have seen John, my son, who now is a super yacht skipper too. I worked out that he is about 3 years older than John. We talked about corruption and asking of monies by officials…which apparently is rife, more so with the big boats. The male officer asked me whether I wanted to take a passenger along to the Azores. My boat is far too small to have a second person on board, which would necessitate extra food and water supplies. Anyway, the easy reply always is to say my insurance would not cover it.

English Harbour was full of super-duper wooden boats that needed a massive crew to sail. Millionaires' toys. I stopped for an ambience lunch. What I had was good but what surprised me was that the owner of the restaurant did not want to show me the bill. Eventually I had a glimpse and then she took it away! It wasn't cheap. I was their first customer and later the place was packed.

A young lad spotted my Jester cap and we started talking, he had nicely prepared a Halcyon 27 and did the crossing with his girlfriend. He put a 'for sale' sign on his boat and he looked very much out of place with those very big, very expensive yachts around. He was preparing to leave for Barbuda and probably leave the boat there. We all know what happened later when hurricane Irma swept through Barbuda.

It was too hot to sleep at anchor in the bay even with the wind scoop fixed on the fore hatch. The heat was probably worse when moored close in the marinas. I think the design of this scoop was not thought out well, as the flexible batten is too long to induce a bend, or may be too thick, or alternately the pocket is too long. The guy who made it never used one and then improve on the design and manufacture. I remember asking Sarah to make me one. She replied that she had never made one, so I copied a few designs from the net and sent them to her but heard nothing. Hence, I bought this from eBay. During the afternoon I used this scoop as a canopy in the cockpit to protect myself from the sun. A bit too small but better than nothing.

While it was cool in the morning I emptied the cockpit locker with the intention of working on the engine. I filled the tank to 7/8 full. I use a marked stick to check the fuel level, no fancy gauges here. I turned the key and the engine fired without hesitation. No fuel starvation. Did someone in St Lucia in my absence syphon my fuel out? Put everything back in the locker. Went ashore and topped up all my spare cans with diesel, 35 litres. Did some shopping and returned to the boat for lunch. I had salmon with fresh salad.

I checked my charts and worked out the distances and courses to the Azores, choices being Horta, Terceira or San Miguel. All dependent on the wind of course as to where I make my landfall.

Monday morning, I had organised for Maurice to come and scrub JABA. Time was passing, and no one had come so I called them on the radio, and four of them turned up on a small Chris-craft, three of them dived under the boat and the fourth operated the compressor on the boat that fed their air on long lines. The guys could not believe that I sailed across the Atlantic in such a small boat, one of them even took his cap off to me. When they finished, I asked them to tow me to the marina and they got me soaked. By now I got wiser about how to avoid getting soaked by rowing ashore only in my pants. I kept my top in the dry-bag together with my camera, laptop, monies etc. I walked up to Shirley Heights and had a late lunch there with superb views of the two harbours. It is a long way up there, and although the view at night would have been spectacular I wouldn't like to do it in the dark, and then have to row to the boat back in the dark too.

I spent couple of mornings at the Covent Garden café with free internet. Most of the big yachts had left, the place looks a bit quieter as it is nearing the end of season. Saturday the Antigua week for the cruisers will start and thereafter everybody will start leaving for home.

I was planning to leave on Saturday, but I thought of bringing my departure forward by a day. As Len says why give the barnacles the option to recolonise you? Also, there is no likelihood that the winds will be going to South East for the next week or so. Apparently Caroline, ex-Britannia skipper, is here and I was invited to a quiz last night but I missed her email. I had missed Terry and Fiona in St Lucia too. Apparently they were in the Bay. I had put a call on the VHF on the off chance but I had no response. It was a shot in the dark.

I heard that Thom had made it to the Marquesas after 38 days. Well done. He had a well-founded Vancouver 28. I took the local bus and went to St John for a bit of change of scenery. There were three cruise ships in port. A hive of activity, there were taxis everywhere. I went for a stroll to the Cathedral which was being restored. Nice commanding position.

Back to the bus station and this time I went to Jolly Harbour. I enquired about a proper little rib at the well kitted out chandlery. Apparently, the fibre glass one is more expensive than the aluminium base one. Far too pricey. Now I see why they get pinched. This place was very expensive, even the Greek restaurant had some eye watering prices. I did not attempt to enter into a conversation in Greek with them.

The amazing yacht 'Maltese Falcon' in Falmouth bay had a Greek guy on board as crew whom I met at the dive shop. We had a bit of a chat and he told me that the boat was owned by a Greek lady, he told me her name but I cannot recall it now. If you can spare 400,000 euro a week to charter it, this is the boat for you.

Antigua to the Azores

I departed in the rain. I used the engine to get out of Falmouth harbour assisted by the genoa. Wind was from the east quadrant and as I could not clear the island after a few tacks I decided to motor-sail to clear the island. A British boat tailed me for a while but turned into the north of the island. I did not have much sleep the first night, a couple of tankers went by. Second day the wind backed a bit, therefore a more northing course. A bronco night followed with some squalls in between too.

On Monday noon, I held the bilge pump handle vertically in the cockpit to ascertain whether the sun is north or south of me. Well I am still north of the sun's zenith, some distance to go to cross the tropic of Cancer at 23.5 N. The seas are calmer and the wind lighter, so I can indulge and play around a bit. I finished reading the second book on this leg, 'Hitler's Canary'. I started with Ewen's book on ethnic cleansing in Croatia, during the 1990s. I think at this rate I will be running out of books to read and I will be reduced to re-reading the instruction manuals afresh!

I developed a tooth ache, lower jaw, right side at the back, this seemed to last for a while. I sipped a mouthful of port and bathed the tooth in it a couple of times in the evening. Well instead of spitting the port and wasting it I swallowed it. This went for a few days the tooth ache vanished but the gout ache on my big right toe returned. I had to abstain from the port for a while until things got back to normal.

About a week after leaving, I noticed that my back was painful and itchy. Did I burn myself in the sun? I am always careful not to expose myself to the sun more than 20 minutes a day. Then it clicked, when I came back from the last dinghy trip to shore, I did not have my top on. I unloaded the dinghy then lifted it on board, packed it and secured it on deck for the trip. All this took some time, much longer then my 20 minutes limit. Easy to forget about sunburn when you are busy on a job.

I was having a lot of problems with the activation of my Iridium air time. It would seem that staff at MailASail in London cannot tell when a contract on a specific date starts. I was left with no connection for nearly seventeen hours. I kept on getting the message 'INVALID ACCOUNT'. On dry land this does not matter but practically anything can happen at sea and you may need an urgent access to contact shore based services. This was not the first-time staff that deal with Iridium service in UK, often do not have their facts right. The firm I was dealing with before, in Poole, were totally hopeless, every week I would be given different information. The guy I had to deal with was not the same one that I made the initial contract with. So, I let the contract lapse and consequently lost over an hour's air time. Then close to the date of the contract renewal, I had the original guy contact me offering a proper renewal, too late by then as I had swapped over to MailASail.

I started having problems with the Marlec HRDi charge controller, and the wind generator. I started experimenting with different set ups in order to get to a favourable outcome, but definitely the wind generator is no longer charging.

I must have hit something during the night, though I heard nothing. At daylight we were hove to and I could see that the self-steering blade was horizontal. I ascertained that there was no damage, so I reset the blade in its vertical position.

Still hot, had a shave and a wash, did some washing, took some video of things happening around me, charged the tablet, the camera battery and the laptop too. Finished Thomas Langer's book in PDF that Len kindly sent me when I was in UK. One good think about books on the tablet is that you can read them during the night without having to put the lights on.

Tuesday 9th of May. 29:28 N 55:52 W. I was awake just after 0500 hours local time, having had a second lovely night of glorious sailing. It is rather chilly this morning, first night that I have had to put a light fleece on. The wind has veered and I am on course.

The winds are variable, I am trying to go as direct as the winds will allow me to the Azores, but it appears that I am going more north than west. The logical route most skippers take is go north and then travel east along the latitude of the Azores, whereas I am on a beat practically all the time. Len sends me messages where the best wind is, but it takes me two days to get there, by which time the forecast is different. 'Grey Goose' a British sailing boat passed me CPA 1.4 NM and during the night a Swiss catamaran and another slow yacht passed by, no AIS and no RADAR. Weather sunny, evenings cool. Tack Tick decided to work, it may have been the relentless heat that was preventing it from functioning. I finished Jackie's cake. I cannot fish as there are too many weeds floating around which leads me to conclude that I must be circling the Sargasso Sea. Yesterday I had to do a pirouette in order to clear the weeds from the steering blade. My last egg turned out to be bad, over the side it went.

The first predicted gale arrived on 13th of May and I employed my survival tactics. VMG poor at 46NM. More or less half way point to the Azores.

Mid May, 33:07 N 47:51 W, wind at 6kt, I decided to put the engine on to chase some clouds and charge the batteries. Today there are whales and turtles, my chores included boat-work, maintenance, personal hygiene and more washing of smalls. It was very cold last night.

I had pasta with artichoke hearts and octopus with Kalamata olives preserved in olive oil, the latter an expensive jar from the 'Epicure' supermarket in Jolly Harbour, Antigua. Next day, I was back to sausages. The black semi-submersible 'container' which I just missed, turned out to be a huge black whale resting. Most of its body was out of the water. Only when it decided to dive I realised that it was a whale! The other three whales that kept circling JABA were showing very little of their bodies above the water, I only managed to photograph their barnacle infested parts of their heads.

'ANAIS' set the AIS alarm in the evening, when the CPA dropped to 5.2NM I called them on VHF and asked for a forecast. For the next 24 hours wind SW 6, this confirmed Len's 20 plus. The cold front arrived with the rain at 14.15 and it was all over by 16.30. But what a scorpion's sting of a storm, the ferocity was unbelievable. I had a napkin sized foresail but I could not keep it as the forestay was behaving like a snake. I call these cold fronts 'the rapists'. The gales tend to be 'the lovers', you know they are coming, staying with you, tease you for a while then they leave you, you survive, you are happy and exhilarated once they have gone. You survived.

I put some Miles Davis on, had spaghetti with mussels for lunch followed with fruit salad. I heard that some of my spots do not reach their destination. Not much good if you are to rely on the spot to act as an EPIRB.

Today's music was Getz/Gilberto. Marinated pulled pork with spaghetti. I am still on Carib time. I'll revert to BST once I reach the Azores.

22nd May, seas very rough, and provoked me back to survival mode. Yesterday had the best run ever. 33NM in 6 hours, I sailed along as if the boat was on rails. Four times that would have given a 132NM run. The wind dropped, and the best run so far stands at 114NM. Winds remained variable, from 31kt down to 14kt. I am concerned about my air time, I am eating into it quite fast, I may need to curtail the blog.

24th of May, I spent some time sorting out the reef lines on the main. The gales ripped off the reef track from the boom. Sacrificed the first reef and lashed the second reef's cringle to the boom. I put a medium sized block to act as an outhaul/second reefing. The set up worked fine, I lost a bit of time in sorting and working things out. Eventually, this set up brought me all the way back to Southampton. Quite a successful improvisation.

Gale number two hit me on May 26, everything went as predicted, gybed at 0400 hours and again at 1530 hours. Cold front followed a bit later. XTE was 15NM. The seas were rough. I also had a scare with a vessel, I thought it was a fishing boat that was coming towards me. No AIS and no radar. I called them on the VHF, dead silence, no response. I switched on my AIS transponder, he stopped moving. I could see by now that he had no fishing gear on board and behind the bridge, a rib was lashed down. I assumed that it must be a coast guard cum fisheries vessel, I could not read the ship's name, which looked over two lines long.

Now that the gale dissipated by early afternoon, according to Len something lively was to follow. Yes, it was a third gale that lasted overnight, and kept me on my toes. The noise was tremendous. In the morning 'Ursula' gave me the forecast as 7-8 for the duration of the day. I was drenched while staying by the companion way, this was the first time this had happened to me on this leg. As I went to change by the heads, a wave lifted the boat up and threw it down to the starboard side. Water came in through the ventilator that is located on top of the fore hatch and drenched me for a second time. The fenders in the cockpit managed to go overboard, the starboard dodger ripped its middle mounting cringles, the rubbish that I kept in a netting twisted out of place. The boat had been pooped. The emergency boarding ladder deployed itself.

There was a mess in the cabin too, everything on the port side lifted and was deposited to the starboard side, cutlery and everything that was loose including my dental partials (prosthesis). I looked for these all day. Lifted the cushions, looked behind and under. I lifted everything from the floor, nothing. I did not really want to lose these even though I do not wear them on board. Went to bed thinking where on earth can they be? I transferred all the rubbish from one bag to another and found some cutlery there but not my teeth. Next day did the whole thing again. On the starboard side quarter berth, I keep a couple of plastic boxes of the type you slide under a bed. They come with a lid. On one of these boxes I keep the log book, a Breton plotter etc. I was looking for something else and opened the box and found on top of the documents kept there, a skin of a light line. Normally this lives by the cooker on the port side, how did it end in the box? Started to look through the contents of the box, boat documents, insurance papers, other official documents and receipts and at the bottom corner I found my partial false teeth. It only took two days of searching to find them. As the boat became 'airborne' the lid must have lifted, the items from the port side lifted too and as the boat slammed down sideways, the port side items found their way across and entered the box, gravity and inertia did the rest and shut the box lid. Amazing. There was more to come. With the impact all the tools that I keep in the drawer by the engine moved and stopped it from opening. No matter what I tried I failed. I looked from the sides of the drawer but had no access. Eventually I decided to solve this once I arrived in port.

I was nearing the Azores, Pico came into view. On the approach to Terceira the wind kept on dropping, big decision do I sail or do I put the engine on? A lot of procrastination ensued. I could not see the island, as it was obscured by clouds. Only when it started getting dark and the lights on the shore lit up did I see the island. I put the engine on, and dropped the hook by the entrance to the marina in Vitoria. I was tired, 30 days at sea, had a beer and a bite and went to sleep.

Praia da Vitoria.

Woke up early, I was the only one at anchor. It was very peaceful, I could hear a rooster from the shore welcoming the day. There was a pervasive smell of cows and dung from the shore. This smell always reminds me of the Fastnet 1991, on the way back, close to land by the Lizard, in the fog without any instruments we could smell the land. Dead reckoning was telling us that the Lizard was ahead, but we could not see a thing. This forced us to tack and head south. Better safe than sorry, especially as I had the safety of my eight crew to consider.

The colours looked very bright and vivid in the early morning sun, for 30 days I had not seen land, yes, I did see Pico and Sao Jorge on the way, but it was hazy and distant. Here and now I had clear cinemascope views.

I picked the hook and headed into the marina, by coincidence Olaf was up and there was a free berth next to him where I stayed for the next three weeks. There were a couple of British yachts that over wintered here. Alex is from Hythe in his boat 'Berwick Maid' a Nicholson 32, with his girlfriend. After three years they are returning back to UK. He has put his boat up for sale at 30.000 euro. Looks quite good, apparently, he painted the boat with commercial vehicle paint that cost peanuts. His girlfriend, a blonde, never smiled or spoke a word not even an acknowledgement, was a yachting magazine contributor. Another couple, also from Hythe, Jane and Michael in their boat 'Isabella of Southampton' invited me on board their yacht but I was far too busy at the time to accept the offer as I was sorting blown fuses etc. They gave me a piece of bacofoil which I used to sort the fuse problem I had. Later, I found out that these fuses were not as rare as I thought. I found packets of them at the Chinese shop. I looked there for a rat-tail saw, to sort out the jammed drawer, they had the blades but not the handle. I could not find anything suitable in any of the other shops either. So, I drilled some holes into the side of the drawer and took one of my hacksaw blades and cut both sides of the drawer, then pulled the front of the drawer loose. Klaus offered me a reinforcing piece of wood but it needed some work, so I called on the marina carpenter who cut me two perfect pieces and told me to glue and screw them too. He obviously had dealt with this sort of thing in the past. The finished product looks as good as new. Klaus also charged my under-sink battery that I had disconnected during the passage as I thought that the solar panel diodes were not doing their job. It took me three days to locate a shop that sold diodes. The shop assistants were extremely helpful, eventually they send me to a repair shop, where they had plenty and they gave me three gratis, and explained to me how to wire them in. The guy was very technical with his language.

Glen and Nancy were in Vitoria. They came to launch their boat. They were staying in B&B initially but once they were afloat they stayed in their boat. Nancy had her birthday and the following day was their anniversary and they spent the day looking to buy a house, which they did. I took Olaf with me and we visited them in their boat for some wine and a chat. Olaf cooked a meal for me again, also we drove to his house out in the sticks for a BBQ with some other French and German yachties. A guy called Rene had bought a three-bedroom house with a pigsty at the back for 80.000 euro within the confines of the town and he showed us around. Glen and Nancy's place is out of town and cost 60.000 euro, not walking distance from Vitoria. They had their Lee designed and manufactured junk sail from China and they spent their time in sorting it out, I took some photos of them testing the sails and boat in harbour. Their boat sailed beautifully.

Out in the bay I saw 'Resort' at anchor. This was the yacht anchored near me in Falmouth Bay, Antigua. What a small world. Beverly and Simon came to the marina in their dinghy and I had a chat with them. Beverly had tooth problem too and I sent her to see Dr Pedro, who had already left for Horta and Dr Monica told her to carry on with the antibiotics.

During probably one of the gales I hurt my knee. I took some tablets to ease the pain. After the first week in Vitoria the knee seized up and I could hardly walk. I called on Dr Denis, the owner of the 50 ft Jeanneau yacht, and asked him in his professional capacity to give me some advice. Arthritis was his first comment, and asked me to take it easy, and get a knee bandage from the pharmacy. Also advised me on my return back to UK to have an MRI scan. I got some Voltarel (Voltarol) gel and took some tablets now and then to calm things down. In time it got better.

I celebrated Corpus Christy with Olaf in Vila Nova, apparently, they have the best festival on the island there.

A couple of days later Guy arrived. I had a number of emails from Norman in Newport, (Rhode Island) informing me of Guy's arrival. I showed him the ropes, laundry etc. We had coffee each morning on JABA, using his coffee and cafetiere. We had a good time together. The forecast was for a storm to hit the island and I was planning to leave once the gale had passed. Things changed though, the gale went north of the island and hit the Ostar participants. One of the boats sunk and the skipper rescued by QM2, others took shelter in the Azores etc. Although we were in the marina and quite some distance from the storm we still experienced a bad night from the noise and the surge. Guy had teamed up with some yachties from Amble and they toured the island on Saturday, and although they drove to Angra, they stayed outside the town. I was asked to join them, but as I had done this trip in 2012 I declined. When they came back they came with the news that there was a bull run in Vitoria in the evening. I joined them for that, but we split once we located the street. I asked for permission to watch the run from the balcony of a private house, whereas they remained in the street and Guy came face to face with the bull. I had to leave immediately after the run as there was a celebration in the Club Nautique. Guy could not remember where the venue was, so he missed the skippers' gathering.

On the following Monday I decided to take the bus and go to Angra. Guy decided to stay for another day as he wished to see Angra, a world heritage town, and came along. In the marina we noticed that Aleko was there with his Nicholson 32. When his wife arrived, they left for Angra. Aleko is from Greece and has been to Patagonia and Falklands too in his boat, sailing solo. The following afternoon the harbour master gave Guy a tow and he was off.

I stayed behind as I had made arrangements with Dr Pedro to have tooth implants. He did some work on my teeth at a very reasonable price, but paying him was a bit of a problem. I checked at all the banks and I had no joy in exchanging my Sterlings. Even Olaf took me to his bank and they said that it would take at least a week to process the monies. I even asked Paolo, the harbour master, but they had no available cash in the marina office and he would not do it through his own bank in case the authorities questioned him, and accused him of drug smuggling or money laundering. I mentioned it to the receptionist at the surgery and she said to me, "Why don't you use my bank?" I tried after the weekend and within minutes I had the euros in my hand and paid my bill. That bank was at the top of the town, I had not realised that there was a bank up there.

Stage one of the implants was successful but I had to stay for a few extra days for my gums etc. to settle down. I was pumped with drugs, there was some swelling and I was given further drugs and mouth washes. I was asked to consume ice cream instead of proper food for a few days and that gave me diarrhoea, and then I had to eat a kilo of rice over the next few meals to calm things down. I asked for Dr Monica to accompany me on the boat and look after me. Had I had a bigger boat it would have been ideal. I followed the instructions given to me on oral hygiene and put updates on my blog so that Dr Pedro could read them.

Three weeks in Vitoria flew by. I managed to add to the Jester Challenge wall painting, Caribbean 2017. Dr Pedro gave a party on his boat and I was invited too. That evening I had three meals, one in town, another meal on board JABA and the third at CUCUGA. Plus, all the drinks too.

I sent a number of emails to Marlec about the wind generator etc. and had a good response. I reset everything from scratch. I had a limited success as after a while the wind charger stopped working again. In subsequent emails I was advised to send it back to them once I got back home.

The last leg, Azores to Southampton

The implants delayed my departure and I lost the wind I was hoping for. The wind on Tuesday was fine but only lasted for about 24 hours and thereafter I struggled all the way back with lack of wind, including in the channel, by Start Point.

I had the company of many whales on many occasions and I had a bit of a scare when one of them crossed my bows, a near miss. Two or three kept circling me for days on end, they were travelling more or less parallel to me. Sometimes they were getting a bit too close for comfort. I kept on looking at my lifejacket and the PLB. My heart during this time kept on missing a few beats. I was scared. I would not be the first nor the last sailor with their boat that had been sunk by a whale.

The light winds helped with my oral hygiene. 'Cosco Indonesia' gave a forecast of 20kt of wind all the way to Gibraltar. Nothing like that materialised, so far only 7-8kt. He must have read out last week's forecast! My appetite increased, could not stop eating. Finished one book and started the second. Kazuo Ishiguro and then Ruth Rendell. Some nights I get no sleep at all, 'SKALA' which I spotted about 13-14NM out was coming straight for me, and did not deviate not even a degree from her COG. As Glen says, the guy on the bridge puts his playboy magazine on the radar and after a while he dozes off. I put the engine on and took avoiding action when both the green and red nav lights came into view. There was not much wind to play around with the sails. Len informed me that there is a gale coming on Tuesday/Wednesday hence his advice to steer 90 degrees as the winds will be stronger further north.

Last night the wind picked up, 28kt, this morning down to 20kt. Quite a few stoppers still around. Finished book four. I had some tinned bacalhau with pasta and peas. When Len sends messages to me to go for Lat 42N or Lat 44N obviously he means that there is more wind there, whereas I assume that I will meet the mermaids and I get disappointed when I do not see them.

Sunday 2nd of July. What a contrast today, wall to wall grey and damp. Very little wind, boat speed less than 2kt. Yesterday it was blue sky all over, not a cloud in sight. Wind 13-15kt abeam, straight on course. I gave myself a haircut with the trimmer and made a mess of it. Took the comb number three off and had another go. I bit better but far too short. Finished the 5th book, PD James's 'The

Lighthouse', you can tell she is aged, the language is very old fashioned!

What a performance, I sailed through a fleet of 8 fishing boats that were zig zagging around. Thank god it was still daylight. This was how I celebrated the 4th of July. At 0445 hours I came across a tanker that was killing time. His speed over ground was 0.6kt. I tacked behind him and two hours later, I reverted back to my course. It was raining, with thunder and lightning. Initially I thought that the navy was on exercises, the flashing was distant as was the rumble. Somewhere in front of me I could see pillars of fire. The lightning was like a power station chimney being alight, a column of fire. It looked spectacular and I was aiming for it. After a while the whole show moved to the east and dissipated. About noon the tanker had his orders and started moving towards France, I was on the Latitude of Bordeaux.

There are many beautiful sunsets and sometimes sunrises too. But the sunsets are spectacular in their colour rendition.

Whales around again, the highest exhalation I have seen so far. My cooking menu is varied, mussels, octopus, dobrada (stew with tripe) and today Sopa da Pedra with an added tin of mushrooms, plus wine. The celebratory drink last night was spiced Rum.

As the winds are light and the wind pilot cannot manage to steer a course, I tried to use the Raymarine autopilot. It would not work, I attempted to calibrate it but it works in bursts of ten seconds at a time. So, I gave up. It is 10 years old and probably it needs servicing. I resurrected the Vuarnet sunglasses from the 80's, they are still brilliant but old fashioned. The Oakleys that I use on the boat are from 2004, but they have had it, even the paint has started to peel off.

It is foggy, I could hear the whales but I cannot see them they must be close. I refuelled while everything was quiet, putting 15 litres in the tank.

Sunday 9th of July. I sailed over to the continental shelf. Very strange experience yet again. Seas very confused, swell all over the place, wind died down for a while but picked up again as the boat crossed the first contour. None of my radios has LW so I cannot get any weather forecast. Meanwhile, I can listen to the radio, read my book. Later, I cleaned the cooker and fixed the main halyard winch. Life goes on whether there is wind or otherwise.

The wind died yet again just short of my waypoint, south east of Star Point. Put the engine on in order to stop going backwards as the tide turned, but it was a bit of a waste of fuel. Wind picked for a while and contemplated of going to Plymouth, distance 23NM, I could be there by 1800 hours in the evening. A day wasted. Then I would have to wait for some wind, all these would delay my arrival to Southampton. I decided to carry on. I drifted up and down with the tide, there was quite a bit of shipping around and I dodged the boats around me. Eventually, the wind picked up and sailed past Portland Bill. There were a number of yachts around in the approaches to Poole. The tide carried the boat up to Hurst Castle, and in order to make it as easy as possible I put the engine on too and the boat was flying. When I reached outside Yarmouth I thought I'd take it easy and relaxed. Dropped the main and carried on with the genoa only. Unbeknown to me Bob, Bill and Denis were in Newtown Quay and were trying to contact me. Roy was coming to meet me but he turned around and headed for home as he did not want to miss the tide. They phoned Len who told them that I do not keep my phone on all the time. By this time, I had already switched off all instruments as well. I was in home waters and I was eye balling my way. This euphoria did not last long and in order to make it up to river Itchen on time I put the engine on again. I berthed alongside the fuelling pontoon for the night, and called Jackie to come and pick me up. I spent the night at home. Returned the next morning, I collected some bulky gear from the boat and loaded them in my car. I moved the boat to the mid river pontoon and spent some time tidying up. When I was ready I asked for a lift ashore from a passing rib. They were going to Cowes for lunch.

The boat stayed in the marina for a while as my trolley at the club was being utilised by another member. He had asked me if he could use it for a couple of weeks in April and I had agreed. It was now July and his boat was still on my trolley. It took another couple of months before his boat was moved to another borrowed trolley so that I could come ashore.

Chapter 7
Reminiscing – Fastnet Races

It was some time in the late 70s that I replied to an ad for a crew. There was a few of us that turned up to join Peter Du Bosky on his Derring Do of Beaulieu, a 43 ft, one off Holman and Pye sloop, built by Phillips in Dartmoor, in 1975/76. We joined as crew with the intention of qualifying the boat and ourselves for the **Fastnet 1979**. We took part in a number of general races in the Solent as well as the qualifying RORC races required. We cruised to France too. I remember jumping off on the return trip to another boat as I could not afford the time off from work. I came back from St Malo on Chris's boat a Contest 33. I came on watch at about midnight and what I saw as I came up will stay with me for the rest of my life. I will not forget the sight of the silvery sea and the moon as we were crossing the narrows between Alderney and Cap de la Hague, doing over 11kt over the ground. I alighted at Cowes and took the ferry to Southampton. This same boat lost its transom by being rammed by a French fishing boat that came to rescue them during the Fastnet Storm. Another time I came back with 'Sea Streaker' a lovely aluminium yacht, I was left on deck all alone on the helm. When the owner came up he was not very pleased when he saw the rest of my watch all asleep. He was Peter's friend, who joined us in one of our trips to Cherbourg when we went to a party organised by the Lord Mayor of London, on board the Lloyd's yacht Lutine. It was during this trip that we ruined the engine in the gale that caught us unprepared (water in the diesel tank) and had a tow in by the French pilots who were demanding a large sum for the service. Peter and his friend managed to reduce this charge as they spoke French and simply gave them a bottle of whisky. In the restaurant the then Lord Mayor of London, Ken, and his wife came and sat on our table. He wanted to know whether I was a practising Christian. How strange I thought, as I had a teacher back in Bristol, in the mid-sixties, who had asked me the same question and invited me to St Mary Redcliffe church to attend a talk after the service. This was given by an

Oxbridge lecturer who had converted to Greek Orthodoxy. I remember my teacher walking me to the front row of the church in front of a full congregation, everyone with their eyes on me.

The Trinity vessel engineer came around to our boat in Cherbourg to look at our engine problem. He bled the fuel line and everything worked. Next morning same problem occurred and despite following the engineer's instructions, I could not start the engine. This prompted me later on to go to Peterborough and attend a short course at Petters about engine maintenance. We had to leave the boat in Cherbourg and take the ferry back to Southampton. This of course stopped us from taking part in that ill-fated 1979 Fastnet. That week I was up at Nottingham University doing an OU course, a module on the 'biological bases of behaviour'. During the storm I was kept awake from the noise of the tree outside our dormitory. Cyril the rat was assisting me in my module and rescued me from participating in that awful event. I never realised how clever lab rats were. I phoned Peter the next day and he told me that some of our friends' boats were damaged and some crew had sadly died. Later in the season, a few of us took a ride on Brian's boat and brought 'Derring Do' back. Brian Stuart, I believe, was a Lloyds man who owned ZULU, designed by Laurent Giles. This boat eventually was sold and its spinnaker, if I remember correctly, had a spear and shield, and was renamed Cetewayo. Brian had on board an early Loran, a hyperbolic radio navigation system, it looked impressive but complicated with the charts having all those coloured hyberbola printed on them.

So, the next attempt was the 1981 Fastnet Race. We kept on sailing and had added some new crew to our core. Peter said that a Turk had applied but did not pick him as he thought that the two of us would not get on. Who knows? It was during 1981 on the way to St Malo that I excelled myself on the helm when I overtook numerous yachts. As a result of this performance Peter then gave me the task of being the helmsman for the Fastnet. We shared the helm between the two of us. Meanwhile I started on a number of RYA courses and qualified as Yachtmaster Offshore. I came to an agreement with Peter whereby I'd pay a fixed sum and use his yacht for teaching the practical side of sailing. I set up a business 'Le Weekend' as a part-time sailing school.

The 1981 Fastnet came and went. I was on the helm coming into Plymouth afterwards when the wind died down, the crew came up, they were having a meal, to sort the sails for me as I started going backwards. Parties and celebrations followed. We decided to take the boat to Fowey afterwards for a break. I asked some youngsters in their sailing dinghies to take me ashore and we started talking about the Round the Island Race and the 1600 boats taking part. One of the youngsters said, "There must be a very long start line." Their experience of starts always included all the dinghies/boats, so the thought of staggered start never occurred to them. I also remember that one of the guys on board treated us to champagne and another to cream tea. I think the latter was by John an ex-army officer. Some years later, I took John with me as crew for a delivery from Mylor to Southampton. I introduced Keith, the son of a neighbour to sailing, but his dad later told me that Keith had a heart problem and he should stay away from sailing. Some years later I asked again, Keith had a lot more available time and he was an asset to Peter. One day Keith went to drop the letters in the post-box in town, fell down and died. It was a big shock. Keith also got involved with the Ocean Youth Club and he met a lovely lady and they fell in love. This romance was not going anywhere as her father objected to the union because of Keith's social and medical background. Really sad. Peter later asked permission to name his launch in the Thames after Keith. Things did not end well with Peter either. He had his own business, a quantity surveyor office in London, and was also a Lloyds underwriter. He 'brushed bums' with Princess Anne as he used to say during dinners. We waved at Ted Heath's boat when we sailed by, he was known to many. But when the bubble burst he had to give up his house in Scotland, the Porsche, the launch, the yacht (sold to a Dutch guy) etc. When I met him on board Queen Victoria during my Baltic Cruise, he opened up and told me about his days as an officer in Hong Kong etc. Now he and his wife live in a small flat in Hamlet Towers. I was invited to go and see him but never followed his offer. He used to be at Swiss Cottage and then moved next door to David Lean the film director, somewhere in the docks. I went there once but I cannot remember much. One of the crew was his friend John who was a newspaper editor and used to get drunk most of the time. Another local guy was John, 'Mr Kipling'. He was the sales director of Mr Kipling and he always used to bring samples for us to try.

A colleague Andy French from the office wanted to charter a yacht and I accompanied him to Britannia Sailing School. While I was there, Pat, Eddie's then wife told me that they needed a skipper for the Easter weekend, without hesitation I said yes. That's how I joined Britannia. I was preparing for the **1985** Fastnet, quite a big thing those days as Roger and Eddie had committed to take 100 crew, train them and then take part in the Fastnet race. We had more skippers than boats. Chris Serle was 'In at the deep end' series. He had to learn all about sailing and skipper the yacht for the race. In fact Ian, an RYA skipper, was on board in the background. I met Chris a number of times, who at the time was also doing a Greek language program with Katia Dandulaki. I was teaching Greek in those days and I was very familiar with the programs as I used them in my classes. Chris asked whether I wanted to be introduced to Katia. I did not proceed with the offer.

I was assigned to be second in command to Peter on an OOD 34, but after leaving the Needles the rudder fell off. Peter (if that was his name) called the RNLI and they towed us to Yarmouth, thus we were out of the race. The rest of the crew, that included a young female psychologist, chose to go to the Channel Islands on a cruise, I declined and took the boat back to Shamrock. In fact, I was towed there by Ian Knight.

1987 was my next Fastnet on 'Hope and Glory' the first of many. The owner, Brian, had leased the boat to Britannia and he wanted to take part with me as a skipper. What a prima donna he was. During one of the qualifying races he refused to take over his watch. It was a bit rough, I was not going to stay up and do two watches back to back, so I asked the helm to go north, from France towards St Cath's, and I went down below for a kip, I had decided to sort things out later. A keen sailor on board Don was not impressed. Later during the Fastnet race, Brian and Don argued all the time and Brian threatened to kill Don if I did not get him off the boat in Plymouth.

While still in Shamrock Quay waiting for our turn to leave, we started the engine but once we put it in gear the boat shuddered as if she was going to fall apart. Brian decided there and then to cancel the race. I pleaded with him about all the effort we put in the last two years and in any case, we did not need the engine other than to charge the battery. Only Ian Knight was left in his Sigma 33 in the marina and he gave us a tow half way down Southampton Water. We sailed after that as normal. After crossing the finish line in Plymouth we had a tow from a Dutch boat, who cast us off just before the entrance to QAB. I had phoned the marina and was given instructions to go alongside a big boat, the crew of which did not want us alongside them. Neither of us skippers had a choice in the matter, the marina was full. I managed to despatch Don before Brian came back on board in the morning as he spent the night out with his girlfriend. We were towed out by one of our Britannia boats, sailed to Dartmouth, and berthed alongside one of our boats. A crew member of the boat next to us donned his wet suit, put couple of tins as a weight in his suit and dived under us to see what had gone wrong. One of our folding prop's blades had sheared off. Same routine of being towed in and out and we stopped in Poole this time. A number of crew kept on leaving our boat, so I phoned home and asked my wife to bring John, our son, to give me a hand. We had a biscuit battle in the Solent among the Britannia boats that followed us.

Fastnet **1989** was not on my list. We had built an extension to our home and that was taking too much of my time and energy, and to recover I decided to go to Morocco alone with Explore, and for the first time I discovered that there was a life outside marriage, children, work and commitments. There was also a me somewhere there. We had overstretched ourselves in more ways than just financially. It was an excellent break which was also the start of cracks appearing in my first marriage. In hindsight, 20 odd years later I think it was a good move.

I took part in all five Fastnet Races in the nineties. The **1991** was brilliant, the crew were all well trained to the degree that when the trailing log packed up, they still looked at it every hour. Two chemists John and Di on board, one teacher and the other in research, Sue a patent solicitor, Frank the Didcot power station manager, Roger an architect/surveyor. Sera an Oxford rowing team member but I cannot remember what she was doing at the time. The last guy Chris was a good karaoke singer. Roger was the bilges rat, he took it all onto himself to clean the floor every time it became an ice rink, which was inevitable as we had a rusty leaking diesel tank. Di's husband, a Colonel I believe, couldn't figure out why I was not taking things seriously. Roger became known as the Bass man too because that was all he was drinking. On the way back near the Lizard we wrapped the spinnaker, then the fog came down, by then we had no log, no Decca, so next stop was France and not Plymouth. First Sera, then I, went up the mast to sort out the wrap. In Plymouth, we went out for a meal and unbeknown to me during the day the crew found an artist who sketched 'Hope and Glory' rounding the Fastnet Rock and all eight of them signed it and presented it to me at the dinner. I had it framed and is hanging at home now in our lounge. The Colonel who was older than Di died soon after and Di started flying lessons. Sue moved to Manchester. I still keep in touch with Roger. He bought a Sigma 362 to go around the world with it, but he discovered he had back problems so he sold the boat and decided to go around the world by flying from place to place. His trip was east to west. Mine a few years later was west to east, though more or less we covered the same ground.

I think Dave in 1991 had Jane as crew on board his boat as well as Linda. Privately Dave bought his own boat a Trident 24 which he sailed single handed to the Caribbean, St Lucia, via Cape Verde, in 1992/93. He sold that boat there. In 1993, Dave did the Fastnet in his own boat a Contessa 32.

Fastnet **1993** was the one that I had to split the crew into smokers and non-smokers. Four on each watch, worked a treat. I asked John what job he would like to do and opted for the foredeck. It was a windy race and John got drenched every time he went on the foredeck. We had engine problems this time, mainly in starting the engine, so I allocated Peter to be in charge of the engine. We were anticipating some bad weather, we rigged the blade, cranked it in with a handy billy and off we went. On this trip we had on board one guy, from Lymington, who was not a team player. Another guy was someone big in the Jaguar Company, and lived his life as if there was no tomorrow. His wife did not approve of his antics and comedy acts, but it was fun to have him around. We were becalmed by the Lizard. Martin Lewis with this crew were about 100 yards ahead of us. I asked my crew whether they wanted to beat them to the finish line and all agreed. We put the spinnaker up and flew it very shy, and beat the other boat by miles. They thought we were doing the wrong thing. We had practised and practised for hours on how to cross the line in Plymouth by dropping the spinnaker very close to shore. There were many spectators ashore both friends and relatives of my crew who commented how professional we looked in our outfits. I had asked them to wear their rugby shirts at the start of the race, put them away during the race and then wear them when crossing the finish line. The guy from Lymington did not want to do it as his shirt was wet but I made him wear something underneath and then put the wet shirt on top. In the restaurant in the evening we started singing Land of Hope and Glory and the other boat's crew took offence to it. When we came to leave Plymouth, we were in Sutton Marina, somehow the Lymington guy jumped ashore at the lock. Half way to the water break, Martin called me on the VHF saying that a member of my crew was left behind. I told him that I was not going back to pick him up and Martin brought him to us instead. Later in the Solent, Martin was ahead of us and as we approached them they started pelting us with fruit, tomatoes and whatever came to their hands. We retaliated, one of my raw eggs landed bang in the middle on someone's chest. Unbeknown to me one of Martin's crew was a videographer and recorded the whole trip including the fight in the West Solent. I have a copy of that VHS tape. Later, Martin bought his own boat and went around the world with his wife. I met him and his wife in Cowes week for the Fireworks display. He now lives in Guernsey.

Fastnet **1995**, I remember this especially for Chris. A tower of a man who at the end of the race wanted to join the RORC. Things had changed with Britannia Sailing, Roger had died, and was being run by Kevin and Kirsten's boyfriend. (I called the latter 'the clerk', he was not liked by the old hands in Britannia). I also remember it as the 'toilet seat' year. I went out several times to do weekend tuition and put on the defects list 'toilet seat', this happened many times but no one was replacing or fixing the toilet seat. As we were going to be away for a week or so on the Fastnet Race with no proper toilet seat, my crew took it upon themselves to remedy the situation and went and bought a good quality toilet seat and presented the bill to Britannia. Anne (the nurse) was on board as was an ex-army officer, plus Jim who had his own boat and was a bit of a loose cannon. Anne was at the helm as we were rounding the Rock in light winds when we became tangled on a lobster pot line. The officer cut the line and Jim went to broadcast to the world our predicament on the VHF. You do not use the VHF without your skipper's permission. Jim later wanted to do his Yachtmaster with Dave in Auriga, a Contessa 32. And as Dave could not spare the time I took the boat out and practiced with him during the day and picked the examiner up in the evening. Jim stayed below and was passing instructions to me. One instruction was incorrect and I questioned it. The examiner gave me a kick to stop me from giving feedback to Jim. Needless to say, Jim failed at that outing.

Chris came around to see me at the Boat Show and told me that he was made redundant and his wife left him saying to him that he was not in a position to look after her in a manner that she was accustomed to. How mercenary wives can be? Such a mild easy-going person.

Fastnet **1997** was quite an entertaining one. John was back, Colin, Helen the vet, Sue the Barrister, Dave her friend and a young lad from Britannia to make up the numbers. We no longer had 'Hope and Glory', and we had moved from Shamrock quay down to Warsash and the boat was 'Knight School' a Dufour 35. On one of the qualifying races we were scheduled to go to St Malo, we had head winds and we were not going to make it there and get back within our allotted time. We had a pow wow and decided to call it a day, just north of Guernsey. I was out voted and instead of going to Cherbourg we went to Alderney. While there I readied myself to eat yesterday's rice when Susan said you must not eat old cooked rice, but I have been doing just that all my life! That was the first time I heard of it. Mind you, she was shocked that I survived.

On the way back from the Rock, we were going all over the place, I suggested to the crew that we could take it easy and reduce sail but as it was a race let's go for it. They agreed. In Plymouth, I had one too many and I do not look so good in the video. From Plymouth to Southampton, Colin would act as skipper as part of his yacht master training. As we left the marina and were coming towards the breakwater, I cut the engine off, I just wanted to see his reaction and how he was going to set sails, navigate etc. He did fine. This created some fuss from the females as they thought that I was being mean. He took a watch and I took the other. He always kept an eye on me in case I produced some more surprises. In the Solent, I filled a bucket with sea water and kept it by the binnacle. Colin asked John why has he done that. John was not any wiser either. My tradition was that when we went around the Rock we cracked a bottle of champagne and offered some to the gods and the crew drunk the rest. I always kept a second bottle for when we re-crossed the start line back in the Solent. So, the water was to cool the champagne. Good to keep surprising your crew.

The Fastnet **1999** was my last one. Again on 'Knight School', I had John Carter again and another John. Also, with us was a diplomat who knew Brian the British Council in Athens, when they were serving together back in Lesotho. Brian before taking the post of British Council in Athens used to come to our house for 3 months to learn Greek. I met him a number of times in Athens. There isn't anything memorable about this Fastnet other than that we were wearing yellow rugby shirts.

I was due to help Terry, of 'Drake's Drum' with the **2001** Fastnet, but I had an operation on my hand (trigger finger) and did not want to push it. So, I had to say no.

Sailing School

With my own 'Le Weekend' sailing school I took out some Doctor friends of mine with their wives. It was fun. Some of them were my Greek language pupils too. Another time I took some other Greek friends out and that was all as I became involved with Britannia and didn't have time for my own business.

Britannia was initially set up in Portsmouth and then moved to Shamrock Quay, Southampton, were I joined them. They were operating from a log cabin at first, then moved to couple of other places in Shamrock Quay, and after Roger's death they eventually moved to Warsash and finally they went bust. Initially they were the two partners Eddie and Roger. Then they decided to split and go their own ways. Eddie asked me to move with him and offered me all the sailing I wanted but I decided to stay put with Roger. I did not look upon Roger as a boss but as a friend. He was pleased with me and I was happy with what I was doing. I qualified as yacht master instructor in 1986 and I was taking out pupils for their exam prep. Most people were OK, occasionally, I came across someone that I could not approve. However, all the years I was there it happened twice. There was one really dangerous Brit who came up from the south of Portugal where he kept his boat, but had no idea about boat handling let alone sailing. He almost killed us in Cowes with his boat handling, and when I asked him to give me a course to steer from Norris buoy to Hill Head he disappeared for at least half an hour. When he came up I had already made the crossing. He invited me to sail with him in Portugal. I value my life too much to agree to this. He would have been a liability in his sailing boat. I told Roger about it, but they still put him through the exam and the examiner failed him. I was told later that the RYA gave him some sort of qualification after some intense discussions. There were a lot of corporate weekends, Round the Island Races, trips across to France, races among us skippers. There was a great camaraderie to all this.

Dave and I were picked a number of times to race. We took an engineering firm for three races in the Solent with a meal in between at Yarmouth on the Saturday night. We stopped for lunch at Cowes. The wind picked up and we started the race to Yarmouth, Dave managed to get there, but my crew could not cope. I was up by the mast and I could smell the vomit, but I could not see it. One of the crew was decorating the back of my wet gear. The owner of the firm, whom I had in my boat, decided that the guys had had enough, so we turned back to Cowes. He hired a taxi and took us down to Yarmouth for the meal and brought us back to Cowes. The following day we had two races which my crew managed to win. They were very pleased with our performance as skippers and sent a complimentary letter. Apparently, Roger classified these letters as raspberries and strawberries. Complaints – congratulations.

A group of friends wanted to go across to France and they asked for two skippers, which is an unusual request. I took one watch and Dave took the other. Dave was very kind to his lot and did most of the work himself. Whereas I treated them as a normal crew and they did all the work themselves.

I took some solicitors with their girlfriends – they would not leave the marina in Cowes unless we had ice on board for the Kir Royale.

Some University lecturers on board wanted to figure out how the tiller worked. You pushed it one way and the boat headed the other. They sat down and tried to solve the problem mathematically, to be honest, I did not pay much attention.

A channel island aircraft pilot with his wife, a banker, asked for a skipper for their yacht to brush up their skills. They were fine really they did not need me. I just showed them a few tricks of the trade, eventually it came to set up the spinnaker which was in a mess, twisted all over the place. I went on deck with the wife and started pulling bits of sail here and there and tried to visualize how to organise it. The surprise comment from the lady was she could not visualise it at all. To her it was just an unsolvable puzzle. The spinnaker went up fine and we snuffed it at the end.

Another time, we went into Cowes for supper, the object being to prepare for a night passage across to Gosport. This was part of a five-day RYA course. The wife of a student asked me if she could take the boat out in the dark, as she could see how everything looked in day time. I had no objection to that. We left our mooring in the dark. The crew took some time to hoist the main and the working jib once we were outside the harbour, by this time the lady had lost her bearings and could not figure out where we were and where Gosport was in relation to us. Many lights surrounded us. There was more to come. After a while, her husband took the helm and we came into Gosport, to what at the time was Camper and Nicholson Marina. A bit more to the left, a bit to the right a bit more power here and there and we moored without any problem, or so I thought. When I questioned how he felt he had performed, he told me that he did not have much night vision and that he was colour blind. He relied exclusively on my directions. Had the occasion arose that I needed to go down below, we would have been in dire straits. After that incident, I asked whether anybody was colour blind or had impaired night vision at the start of every outing. I remembered this incident only last week when I met a friend at his club and he mentioned he was colour blind.

I went to see my son John at Falmouth (1991-1992?) when the super yacht he was working on, stopped for a break, on the way to Germany for a refit. I was picked from the shore by a rib, its tubes were as tall as me. Then a fog set in as thick as a pea soup. They needed to go ashore and pick up an officer, but how to do that in a thick fog? John and another deck hand got in the rib and one of them held a huge baking tray high above his head. I was in the bridge looking at the radar screen together with a number of officers who were guiding the rib by way of the VHF radio which way to steer for the shore. It was brilliant. I would never have thought of that. Radar at that time was an unknown entity to me.

It was during this time that Alex Thomson (Hugo Boss) joined Britannia as a shore maintenance crew. Later, he qualified as skipper and partook in our races. After Roger's death for a time he run Britannia from Warsash. I remember when he phoned and asked me to go out with the sailmaker to sort out all the new sails they were buying for the fleet. I teased him by saying, why me? Who told him that I could sail? Some of the youngsters of Britannia used to bet on us skippers who was to come first at the weekend races. I was told this years later by Dave who by then had grown up and came to work for me at the Southampton Boat Show, a brilliant boat handler. He was also the one that heard that someone was after my position as manager at the Show. That was at least 3 years before I ceased to work there.

One weekend I was asked to go to Hythe marina and take out a Gin Palace for the day. The owner Linda and a number of her friends were waiting for me. I could only do the Saturday that weekend but I offered to come the following weekend and do the other half of the tuition to which they agreed. As we were passing the Fawley refinery, on the first Saturday, I noticed someone on a stationary powerboat waving his arms up and down. I told Linda that the crew in the speed boat were in distress and asked whether they were willing to help. They were, so we turned around and towed the boat to Port Hamble. I think the boat was an offshore power boat, a racing machine, something like cougar. I went many a times after that to take out Linda and her family boating. When I could not, for example Cowes week firework nights, I would send my friend, Andy French. I remained friends with Linda and Ken, her partner. This was the period before, during and after my divorce from Aria, my ex-wife.

Among incidents that spring to mind are, the nurse from London whom I sent on the foredeck to clip the headsail on. She was taking too long to do it, so I went to investigate. There were two D shackles and she could not figure out why there were two, and which did she need to use. I simply said that one of them was spare. Her next move was to throw over the side the 'spare' shackle she was holding. My jaw dropped to the deck.

This is not the first time something like this happened. I have had to be ever so careful what I say and how I say it. Peter told one of his crew to drop the anchor over the side, the guy did as he was told, but the anchor had no line attached to it. A good anchor lost.

Similar one happened to me, when we arrived at Bembridge at a middle pontoon. My crew jumped ashore without taking a line to tie the boat. I was up on the bridge, rushed down and threw the line, then I realised that the line was not attached to the boat. Even experienced sailors make silly mistakes!

A banker from somewhere in the Gulf States and Ann – a lady dentist were on one of our trips. I sent them on the foredeck to sort out the headsail. They were taking their time. I decided not to interfere, let them sort it out themselves. Maybe they spent more than half an hour, but they solved the problem without my interference. Both were very pleased with themselves.

The dentist had sailed with me a number of times. During the Fastnet race she put her foul weather gear and kept it on for 6/7 days. Slept, ate, stood her watch in the same outfit. What she did behind closed door in the heads I do not know.

I had a young lad on board, a pilot, came to me and asked permission to go down below as he was feeling queezey. There was a job that needed to be done and I told him he was the right person to do it. He complied, finished the job and afterwards came and said that his mal de mar had vanished.

I knew Richard since he was a teenager, studying in Portsmouth. Came with me a few times, became a skipper, he chartered boats from Britannia entered races. So, when he needed a skipper I would oblige. One weekend I took eight of his Portsmouth Poly friends sailing. Saturday was blowie, so we reefed the sails accordingly and we were fine. We stopped for lunch in Cowes and some of the crew approached me and asked me for a more exciting sailing experience. I took them at their word. We shook all the reefs and went out for more sailing, waves were hitting us from everywhere, we were getting drenched, it was very exciting. We all had wet weather gear, so it did not matter. We stopped for our evening meal back in Cowes and half the crew left the boat and went back to mainland. Excitement, it seems is not for everyone. You may seek it, but it may not be suitable for you.

A party of young grads came one weekend, they wanted to go across the Channel. I checked their experience levels and I think only Kathy had been on a boat before, and I made her the watch leader. We went to Cherbourg and then to Alderney. The passage back to UK was going to be rough, so while we were in Braye Harbour we put a third reef on the main and left. Not long after I was sitting on the companion way and all of them were in the cockpit behind me. After a sudden/accidental gybe the main ripped right across the third reef. I looked behind at their blank faces. I said nothing and turned around as nothing had happened. Eventually I asked them when they were going to drop the mainsail down. We sailed back on the headsail alone. Alison was sick and I told them that they should hold her while she was feeding the fish. The same group kept on coming back for more sailing with me. One of the guys was learning Japanese at the time. They were young bright people. Later Kathy became a skipper with Britannia. I see her now and then with her partner/husband.

One weekend I was given a Sweden 36, belonging to a titled individual and I was asked to take a small group out. The weekend was going to be rough. I took, John, my son to help out. We ended up in Hamble and by Saturday the wind had picked up, to a six. I had on board the manager of the Marriot Hotel in Athens, who owned a yacht which he kept in a marina in Piraeus. He was concerned that we were going out sailing in such poor weather. I explained that I had to go through a syllabus and anyway how was he to learn how to cope with bad weather if he did not experience it? Off we went practicing man overboard etc. He was most impressed, he was shouting 'Jeronimo' as the waves were washing over us. I used to shout 'Jeronimo' myself when I was dinghy sailing in bad weather.

In 1995, during one of the Fastnet qualifying races we lost the wind just north of Cherbourg for over a day. We just drifted across the Cotentin Peninsula with the tide. The crew were pleading to give up and go ashore for a meal and a drink. I refused to budge, I had to qualify the boat and the crew. When we ran out of time I put the engine on and we motored back to base in Southampton. I sent my log book to Alan Green, who was the racing officer of RORC and explained the situation. He accepted my course of action and counted the race as a qualifying one. My crew wanted to rectify the situation and chartered 'MAIDEN'. We left Southampton midnight one Friday and sailed, from Ocean Village to Cherbourg with an easterly wind, we did this in 9 hours. The same easterly brought us back home in 9 hours too. That was a very respectable time. The owner of the boat came with us but he did not get involved with the sailing. My crew wanted me to be the skipper and I obliged. A good time was had by all.

During my training week as RYA instructor, I was with a lovely bunch of individuals who took a few liberties in their approach to sailing. Everyone had allocated jobs, like watching the depth gauge and shouting the moment you thought the boat would touch ground. We tacked our way up narrow creeks. We had the spinnaker up while going through growing field of rushes, and then another time sailing up a dead end under spinnaker and dropping it the last moment. Even did 360 degrees spins with the spinnaker up. This latter became my signature piece. As and when the conditions were right I also did it on 'Hope & Glory'. The crew loved it. The skipper of the boat (our assessor), had taken part in the Fastnet 1979 and had to abandon their yacht, they were rescued by a French yacht. The French skipper asked them to go down below and sit it out. There was a young lad with them in his underpants, apparently, he was asleep when they prepared to abandon their yacht, he kept on passing out from hypothermia. This was a yacht from the National Sailing Centre.

Eventually I gave up teaching sailing. It meant I had to keep up to date with First Aid, and all sort of other things. It also became expensive as I could not afford the time to go out. I was doing it for fun with Roger, after his death it became a chore. Afterwards I was traced a number of times through the net and asked to skipper corporate events.

For a while, I also demonstrated boats to prospective buyers. If they asked for a skipper from the agency the going rate was £150, whereas I would go for a couple of hours for half that amount. There was a lady in Chichester marina I believe who kept on calling on me and paid me well. However, I questioned the prospective buyers as to why they were going for a particular boat, when they could buy something different that would be more fun to sail. I think some of that must have filtered back and my demonstrations stopped.

One guy managed to find my telephone number, probably from that lady, and asked me to skipper for him after buying the boat I had demonstrated to him. A lovely little thing, Etap 26.

I had a firm of quantity surveyors that were interested in the Round the Island Race, they kept on coming year after year. Quite a good bunch of people. One year they inscribed all our names on the tankard that RISC gives to the participating skippers and handed it to me. I have a collection of tankards from these races. I would have had one more but one of the crew one year opened my bag and took it. Though during which year which crew took it I do not recollect. I even have a tankard given to me by Dave with the inscription Basil Basil Basil. We used our own names to call each other while participating in one of the Fastnet Races, so that we did not give away our whereabouts. Even nowadays a small group of us greet each other that way. Trevor Trevor Trevor, has converted to motor boating now.

Groups from 'Marks and Spencers' was another corporate annual event. I remember that one year I forgot to take my tie with me and resorted using a sail tie with my shirt and blazer.

Dave was working for 'Ernst & Young' and I was always one of their skippers at their annual corporate events.

One year Britannia ran out of yachts, so I was given another boat and skippered employees from the Abbey Road Studio. We came last in all the races we took part in. It was a great fun to sail with them as some of their comments were hilarious. I just could not make that particular boat go. I had specialised too much with the Sigma 36, I had sailed them over 10 years. I was not much good with the Sigma 33 either. I liked the 36. Abbey Road Studio engineers came down again the following year, and they must have been the organisers as our boat was the committee boat and we had to lay the course etc. I was invited to visit their Studio in London and I took John, my son with me. It was quite a privilege to be invited. We spent a whole day there. I was filmed by their video department while I was there but I have not seen the results. They gave me a recording of Maria Callas as souvenir, a stamp at the back says 'not for sale'. The only name I remember from that time is 'Lou' the PA to the boss.

I was sent to Lymington to take out a yacht owner for yachtmaster preparation in his boat. Anne an Italian young skipper that worked for Britannia at the time was to take the exam too. Apparently, the owner had theory tuition by another Britannia skipper and was now absolutely out of his depth with the navigation. He was an experienced sailor, the yacht he bought new that was exhibited at Earls Court. He had sailed extensively but had no formal qualifications. I explained to him to forget what he was taught the week before and carry on with his navigation skills as he knew. We practised boat handling for two days, the sat the exam and they both passed. No one has monopoly to navigation methods. As long as you can get from A to B safely you can use whatever method you are accustomed to. Nice guy.

Another yachtmaster preparation was with Roger's army/navy friend. Colonel/Admiral I do not remember. What I remember was when I put him in a tight spot and he was taking his time to sort out the boat, I asked, "To him do you want me to help you?"

His reply was, "Let me figure it out myself." After the 1995 Fastnet Race, there was to be a Round Britain Race and Roger picked this guy as the skipper of the boat instead of me. I had managed to put on board Peter and Dave, two of my Fastnet guys and somebody else had the pleasure of doing the race. Well sometime that's how the cookie crumbles. They were forces mates.

Chay Blyth used to come around to Britannia, I met him a few times. We used to train at times some of his crew. One day I asked him to sign his book for me. He said to me that the book had his name on it, why on earth did I want his signature? I said to him that his signature is the real thing not the one embossed on the book. He obliged, I still have the book.

There were a lot of little things that stick in mind. I was a bit of a pioneer in those days. I often had all female crews unlike my contemporaries. For some unknown reason they were always given to me. I have hundreds of photographs but no names.

Boat Shows

Peter Peacock was a Grecophile. He was a student of mine attending my Greek classes. He was also the manager of the Southampton Boat Show. He used to give me complimentary tickets to attend the Show in the 1980s. At the show, he used to fly the Greek flag and the Greek ambassador used to send him pecuniary support which he had freedom to spend any way he wished. Peter knew that I was involved in sailing, and in 1990 when Richard, his son, was not available to manage the Show marina, I was drafted in as a replacement. It was quite a tough year. Peter was an excellent manager. The following year when I was asked to do it again, I told him I could but only on the condition that I brought in my own crew. He agreed and I engaged skippers from Britannia and others, like Paul, a student, who in 1990 was a security guard at the marina entrance and asked if he could join me instead. Paul had a break in between but I had him back again. He is still a safety boat skipper to this day. I had a female skipper from Britannia and a couple of female ex-students guards that came over to the security ribs over the years. Pioneering stuff in those days.

When I first started as marina manager the entrance to the marina was through a door surrounded by a big tableaux, that hid the two portacabins, one for the Marina Manager and Marina Crew and the other for the Walcon on site crew with their tools. There was a double decker bus that housed Alan Lambourn who manned the public address system. We enjoyed each show.

The Southampton Boat Show was bought by the London Boat Show and eventually Peter was made redundant. He was replaced by Richard Mortimer, the London Boat Show manager from Earls Court, and subsequently a number of top brass came and went all with different takes to the show. They dispensed with the tableaux and the entrance to the marina was opened with a free forecourt like space. I suggested that palm trees be placed either side of the marina entrance. Instead a short palm tree was put just outside my office. Some years later that idea was developed by the marketing department, they used sand and palm trees and created a special area which was allocated for children to play in.

Richard eventually set up his own business in power boat tuition. He had a Nelson, and Jackie and I were invited to go out with them. He was married to TC at the time. Jackie was on the helm and forgot to be sick. We went from Port Solent to Chichester for lunch on board and back.

Things were changing in the marina and the show in general, in Peter's days, a yacht that approached the marina could not enter the inner basin to take its allocated space as its draft was in excess of 2.4m. I relayed the information to Peter who told me to tell the skipper to take his boat away. Apparently, that did not go down very well with the skipper and the new management. So, the decision was made by higher management to partially dismantle the marina to allow the boat in and then the walkway was reassembled. Electricity and water supply had to be disconnected, extensions made and then reconnected, a lengthy process. From that time on, it became practice to leave a section of the marina open to allow bigger and bigger yachts to enter the basin and then close it to secure the marina.

After Richard the next manager was Murray who used to be Peter's second in command in the early days. He knew very little about boats. I have just read in the press that he has stepped down for personal reasons.

The Boat Show in London which was originally in Earls Court moved to Excel to accommodate the increasing size of boats wanting to be on display. Unfortunately, attendances plummeted and the show has now been reduced to five days and runs in parallel with other shows at the same time.

Under Murray it appeared that the Show was running mainly under the Health and Safety manager. This led to the end of my involvement with the Show as the Risk Assessment Manager wanted a mate of his to manage the marina.

I was not the easiest person to manage and I had a number of clashes with some of the permanent and part time staff over the years. Seventeen years managing the marina was a long time. This was a blessing in disguise as it freed me to pursue travelling and later my sailing adventures.

Orchids

At work in my office, I always had plants. In 1989 when we had our extension at home I had asked the builder to build me a base for a greenhouse. The base was a couple of feet high onto which the greenhouse is secured. The ground is also dug deep so that there was both a very good height and volume to the greenhouse. I dismantled that greenhouse and took it with me when I moved out after I divorced my first wife. I moved it again to this house after I moved in with Jackie.

During a weekend in the 1990s, I had some consultants on the boat. One of them had been to Borneo, and climbed Kota Kinabalu. I felt jealous, I had to go there. So, in 1995, I bought an air ticket and a Lonely Planet book for Malaysia and left. No plans, no bookings, no nothing. Arrived in Kota Kinabalu and met a couple of German teachers at the airport, we teamed up and went to stay in one of the hostels. They knew of orchids but their itinerary was different to mine. We spent a day together and asked a fisherman to take us and leave us on an island and then come back and pick us up at the end of the day. That was the first time I burnt my back snorkelling: I always wore a 'T' shirt after that.

I went to the national park, booked accommodation there and found a guide for the climb too. Elaine asked me whether she could share my guide and later a German lecturer from California asked me the same thing. So the three of us, plus the guide, formed a nice close knit group. It was there that I saw the smallest orchid. A green clamp stuck on a rock with some very small white flowers, the size of a pin head. You could not really see anything with bare eyes. The tallest orchid was in the same area, 30 ft up a tree. You knew there would be some flowers there but you could not see a thing. Higher up the mountain the guide took us off the track and showed us some big pitcher plants. Rats could quite easily drown in them. We also passed a very eerie patch of stunted forest with Spanish moss hanging from everywhere. The sort of place you could easily imagine that Dracula was waiting around the corner.

Rafflesia was the biggest flower we came across, though it is not an orchid. We came down, stopped for a night at Poring, where there are hot springs and the next day we went our separate ways. I went to Sepilok to see the Orang Utans and stayed in Sandakan overnight. I flew back to Kuala Lumpur for another 11 days. I met a Chinese lady who had a nursery and orchids for sale. We made arrangements for the cities certificates and I took the orchids home with me, which I added to my collection. I made a side trip to Malacca where I had one of my most memorable meals and Singapore for a few days.

I wanted to go to Thailand to look for orchids. After my first marriage ended I purchased my own property and set up my greenhouse afresh. There was also a conservatory at the back of the house which I filled with orchids. I joined Peter's group in 1996 and we had a lovely time driving around Thailand looking for orchids in the wild as well as in nurseries. An amazing trip cum holiday, with excellent company. To do justice to this trip I'd need to write a separate book. I had a dendrobium in my office that I cherished. The white flowers were thinner than a cigarette paper. In Thailand, I saw it in the wild up a mountain in a ditch. What a contrast.

Back home I joined a number of clubs, went to exhibitions, bought more and more plants. Went all the way up to Chatsworth House, where I met Eleanor Bron at the flower show. What a lovely lady. With the Paphiopedilum Club I went to Jersey to the Eric Young Orchid Foundation. It was just our group there, we had the place all to ourselves.

I had over extended my collection, so I started sell some of my collection, particularly, as I had mainly species which are more difficult to look after. I sold some to a banker from Bournemouth who came around to see them before buying. He was a wine connoisseur, nothing less than £45 a bottle was his tipple. Then a guy who had a nursery came around and took the majority of them. Some I gave away some I took to the office, and then it was time to move again. I had an excellent period of learning and enjoying orchid plants. I am still in touch with Peter in Thailand.

During my world trip in 2004, I went to spend Christmas with Peter in Chiang Mae. His house is in fact in Mae Tang. On Boxing Day, we watched the tsunami on his TV. I had to change my plans and instead of going to the western part of southern Thailand I went to the east, Koh Tao Island for the New Year celebrations.

May be sometime in the future before too long, I should write about my round the world trip plus the other journeys I have made in the last 30 years.

Chapter 8
Jester Symposiums, Dreamers and Pogrom

I suppose we all start as dreamers and at some stage, these dreams sooner or later become a reality. To coin a cliché term as they say, money rich-time poor or time rich-money poor. We are all somewhere stuck along this continuum.

Although the sailing team I joined in the late 70s early 80s offered me excellent sailing opportunities I was unable to take much time off of work as I had a wife, children, mortgage etc. to look after. Many in the Jester group are having the same dilemmas and restrictions whether being young or not so young.

Some of us are pecuniary comfortable, inherit some money, from savings or borrowing and we manage to get afloat. But there is a lot more than that. John Tason one day told me that it is not everybody's cup of tea to go Ocean sailing and stressed that he liked it and it suited him. However, after taking part in an ARC, job and family commitments have grounded him.

During the 2014 Jester Challenge in Plymouth, a guy was going around asking questions how he could get afloat and compete at the highest level on a budget of £100. He stayed with me on and off for a long time, presumably he was asking the same questions to others too. I do not know whether he was serious about the sailing challenge or to achieve getting a boat for minimal outlay or perhaps for nothing. Slowly his budget grew to £1000, it can be achieved with hard work over a long time. Everything is feasible. I was having problems with making the Iridium communicate with my 'MailASail' and therefore I had to cut my involvement with him. When I mentioned this to Tony he simply said, "Another dreamer."

We all get inspiration from others, but this 'dream' at times may be unattainable to some, irrespective of pecuniary affluence.

One example is the Golden Globe Race. John Apps some years back set up on the web the Golden Globe Challenge in a manner that the Jester Challenge is run. Do your own thing, stop if need be, no restriction on boat sizes or makes, etc. He had no serious participants, nobody was prepared to join him. However, the GGR stole the show, and people joined it because of the publicity. Marketing is a big business. The first retirement took place within a week. No physical damage to the boat or skipper, we were told. A good thing no one was hurt or injured. A dream too far? A simple realization of the big task ahead? There is however a similar 'challenge' as supposed to a race currently going on, similar to John's with starting points from all over the place, either side of the Atlantic, and with different starting times. It is for people who have similar aspirations and dreams unrestricted by man-made rules. So much like Jester.

At our Jester meeting in November 2012, organized by Tony in Plymouth, us newbies who had completed the Azores Challenge earlier that year, were presented with our green Jester ties. Not all that attended the seminar and discussions in the afternoon, had stayed for the dinner and the presentation. The weather that weekend was extremely bad and had hampered attendance.

The next two Jester meetings were held in Ipswich organized by Paul. It was during the one in 2015, that I sat opposite Roger Taylor. The conversation drifted into the subject of 'refugees' and I made the comment that I was a refugee too. We discussed how he was in Istanbul in early sixties when things were a lot different and very beautiful, and how the Greeks in 1964 were expelled from Constantinople. 12,000 Greeks with Greek nationality were given a 24-hour notice to leave the country. The rest of us, about 125,000 with Turkish nationality chose to leave too in fear of our lives. I was one of those that left in May 1964, I was at the time at the University of Istanbul studying Geography, so it was not much of a problem for me to get a ticket and leave.

This is a long story and this not a place to elaborate further, though a number of my friends have written books about all our problems while living in Constantinople, present day Istanbul. In my lifetime we had the pogrom of 1955. I was a young boy hiding behind the fridge with my parents when Turks brought in from other areas 'hire a mob' started destroying shops, businesses and churches. I could hear the window panes being broken, including the church clock face opposite us. Rapes, deaths, desecrations, digging up the dead, assaulting priests, etc. followed in other parts of Istanbul. The rumour was that the following night they were going to slaughter us all. My father went to see whether his shop was ruined or not. He must have walked at least 4/5 miles, and not once did he step on the road or pavement. He was walking on destroyed clothes, shoes, cereals, food of all description, sunglasses anything you can think of. My father's premises were in a Turkish market place area and somehow survived. Many families after this left for Greece. One of them was my uncle, my mother's brother, who had a young daughter, they considered it not a suitable environment for a young girl to grow up in. Things calmed down and life continued reasonably peaceful until mid-sixties. A second exodus of the Greek population followed, but not all of us that left went to Greece, there are many in USA, Australia, various countries in Europe and like me there are quite a few of us in UK. I renounced my Turkish nationality on the principle 'if they did not want me, I do not want them' and I used to travel with a **laissez-passer** travel document issued from the Home Office in London. The initial one was a folded paper, the second one like a brown passport. Afterwards I applied and became a British citizen.

The following is from a high school friend of mine, Simeon, living now in Texas USA, which illustrates how all of us managed to survive through a misfortune. I picked these comments from Facebook and of others who added to his entry.

Simeon: Fifty years ago today, I boarded an Olympic Airlines plane headed to the USA with a one-way ticket and $300 in my pocket. I had made the decision to never go back to my native land and to face whatever difficulties were waiting for me in my new home. I had some relatives in other places in the US but I headed to Philadelphia all by myself. I had arrived having been accepted to graduate school at Penn but with no scholarship and no guarantee that I will be able to pay so I can be enrolled. I could not expect any financial help from home, so I had to figure out a way to take care of myself. With the help of people that I met in Philly, I borrowed $900 from Girard Bank for my first semester tuition (yes, it was only $900 for a whole semester!) and the rest is history.

Simeon: Thanks Basil. I have been following your adventures with some envy, although I doubt that I would have had the courage to do what you did.

Jacob: I will reach my 50 years mark in January 2019. Same more or less story. The max 'doviz' (foreign currency) of $200 in my pocket and a rather large bag. But, thank God, I had an offer for assistantship from Notre Dame. Tuition remission and $300 a month.

Fedon: Congratulations my dear friend. Same story, year 1972 with $1000 in pocket headed to Washington DC as a foreign student. With two bags of which one had 30 packages of Priatene tablets for

Asthma. I have never used a single tablet since I arrived because it was allergic symptom due to a specific bug which was in the Turkish soil/air... the rest was a life time agony with some successes and some failures. My family was dirt poor and I had no place to turn for a little help.

Harry: Congratulations Simeon and fellow Constantinopolitan. I am proud of you and those others who followed similar paths. Our resilience and determination has served us well. We will always stay close to our roots while continuing to promote our values and traditions which are molded in the centuries long history of our people. I wish you continued success.

The following is from Ted's book, 'Born to Travel', a pharmacist based in Canada. Theofanis Halkusis was seated in front of me in the class at our last year in High School, the Classics stream. We had a science and commercial stream too. I have fond memories of that last year and especially our Christmas Carols overnight singing. A rich Greek had given us a caravanette and a driver for the occasion and we sang our hearts out. Ted had an accordion and somebody else had a guitar if I am not mistaken. Ted's book is worth reading, especially the excellent photographs in it from all over the world. Below are some excerpts which highlight the difficulties I and my fellow Greeks experienced:

"I was born in Istanbul (Constantinople) and grew up during difficult times. Travelling was not a priority for a Greek Orthodox boy growing up in Muslim Turkey. We were not permitted to speak Greek in public nor could we wear Christian symbols such as a cross. Our Greek school uniforms were different than the Turkish ones and we felt compelled to stop wearing them in order to avoid being the target of abuse by the Turks. Going to church on Sundays was always risky and several times we had fights with the Turkish kids. Our Saturday parties had to end before dark and a group of us would have to escort the girls home. I was involved in several fights and still have the scars as a reminder.

I got my first taste of travelling in Anatolia when I was 14. While we were driving on a dirt road with my dad and another couple, we tried to pass a small truck. There were some women sitting at the back of the truck, dressed in black and with their heads covered. The truck stopped abruptly, and several men leapt out yelling and accusing us of following their women. My dad's friend was the driver, with his wife sitting right next to him, but, since arguing was not the wisest option and they were getting more hostile by the minute, we got scared, made a U-turn and never made it to Ankara. The excitement of travelling was replaced by fear. I realized that even travelling was not safe in Turkey.

I attended the Zografyon Greek high school in Istanbul. Every year during Greek Easter, it was the tradition for the final year students to visit the Island of Imvros and celebrate Easter. Imvros, at the time, was the only Turkish island that had a large Greek population and had remained relatively untouched by the Turkish brutality.

After finishing high school, I left for Greece to attend the University in Athens. Since this was the first time that I had travelled outside of Turkey, I was nervous but extremely excited at the same time. I arrived by bus to Thessaloniki where suddenly, everyone was speaking Greek! Here I was free to speak my own language anywhere, anytime, for the first time!

During the 1930s, the Greek population in Turkey was around 125,000 but tension between Turkey and Greece greatly affected their ability to reside in Turkey. By the 1950s, things got worse. The Istanbul riots were organized mob attacks, directed primarily at Istanbul's Greek minority. On September 6, 1955, a Turkish mob that had been trucked into the city in advance, assaulted Istanbul's Greek community for nine hours. As a result of severe beatings, over a dozen people died during the attacks. During these riots, Greek houses were burned, churches were vandalised and women were raped, shops looted and even dead bodies were dug out from the Greek cemeteries. Our apartment was spared, but my father's import-export business was burned down.

The police, who supported the attacks by preparing and organizing the operations, were ordered to hold a passive stance and leave the mob to roam the streets of the city freely and commit atrocities against the civilian population. The violence continued until the government declared martial law in Istanbul and called in the army to quell the riots. The attacks greatly accelerated emigration of ethnic Greeks from Turkey, and the Istanbul region in particular. In 1964, Turks started deporting roughly 12.000 ethnic Greeks who were without Turkish citizenship. The remaining Greek population with Turkish citizenship was facing excessive taxation and other oppressive measures, and was gradually forced to leave Turkey. The once flourishing Greek community was fading away and today there are less than 2,000 Greeks left in Istanbul."

Ted had the same problems as most of us at the time. After finishing his studies in Athens, he renounced his Turkish citizenship and became stateless. After two years he managed to get a Laissez Passer valid for 3 months and for one trip only to Canada. As he says in his book: '*This was probably the best decision in my life.*'

There is another book written by my friend Foti Jean-Pierre Fotiu, a Constantinopolitan, whose family emigrated first to Belgium and then to the States. The book called 'CONSTANTINOPLE, The beautiful city and the destruction of its Greek, Armenian and Jewish ethnic communities'. This is published in the States, I have not read it, but I am sure it is a learned treatise.

I included the above to show of the ethnic cleansing that took place at the time. The remarkable thing is that Ian Fleming, of the James Bond fame, was a spectator during the pogrom of 6th September 1955, watching the developments in the High Street of Pera.

I do not dwell on the past and most of my friends here in England are unaware of these early years of mine. They know I am Greek and it starts and ends there.

I had second thoughts whether I should include these excerpts in a sailing book, but during the long dark nights, in passages you get flash backs, you reminisce and relive your past. So, on balance it felt appropriate to include them.

I came to England with the help of Brian Williams an Oxford graduate whom I met in Theologiki Chalkis, (a boarding ecclesiastical academy) where I was in the high school section for two years before transferring to Zografyon.

I married a young Greek of refugee background in 1970. Her grandparents came over to Greece in 1923 during the exchange of populations, ethnic cleansing. We had two children here in Southampton, my daughter is an Oncology Consultant living in UK and my son a Superyacht skipper who has settled in Spain. We divorced in 1995 and I met Jackie in 1997, we moved together in 1999, got married in 2003 and miraculously she hasn't divorced me, despite severe provocation by virtue of my long absences travelling and sailing.